The Death
of Progress

THE
DEATH
OF
PROGRESS

by Bernard James

ALFRED A. KNOPF   New York   1973

THIS IS A BORZOI BOOK
PUBLISHED BY ALFRED A. KNOPF, INC.

Copyright © 1972 by Bernard James

All rights reserved under International and Pan-American
Copyright Conventions. Published in the United States by
Alfred A. Knopf, Inc., New York, and simultaneously
in Canada by Random House of Canada Limited,
Toronto. Distributed by Random House, Inc., New York.

Library of Congress Cataloging in Publication Data

James, Bernard J.
　The death of progress.

　Includes bibliographical references.
　1. Civilization, Modern—1950–　　2. Progress.
3. Technology and civilization.　I.　Title.
CB428.J35　1973　　901.94　　76–171154
ISBN 0-394-47551-8

Manufactured in the United States of America

FIRST EDITION

To my wife, Betty

"The grave dissociation of past and present is the generic fact of our time. . . ."

—JOSÉ ORTEGA Y GASSET

Contents

Acknowledgments

I WOULD LIKE to acknowledge the critical assistance and encouragement of those who have been particularly helpful during the preparation of this manuscript: Roger Beaumont, Keith Caldwell, Robert Golembiewski, Rainier Hiltermann and Edward Kamarck. I owe special thanks to my Assistant, Margaret Johnstone, for her untiring aid in revisions of the manuscript.

Introduction

THERE ARE SEVERAL REASONS for writing an introduction to a volume such as this. One is traditional, to make a pre-emptive strike on potential critics by suggesting that literature in the field is generally poor and that almost anything would be an improvement. This is a dangerous tactic, since it may stir an otherwise sympathetic reader to critical alert. Another reason is humane. It gives the reader an idea of what to expect and makes it possible for him to decide, while there is still time, whether or not to get involved in the book.

This book is organized in three parts: an opening section that sketches the problem of the idea of progress as a cultural strategy; a middle section that tries to indicate the nature of the evidence for the death of the progress ideology; and a final section that examines the alternatives that face us as a consequence of the collapse of the ideology. Originally the book was intended to concern management, but it soon became apparent to me that unless I examined the larger events taking place about us, talk of managing our way out of our difficulties would be idle. For we must try to understand what is happening to us before we can pretend to try to manage our way out of our predicament. The predicament is clear enough. We live upon an overcrowded and pillaged planet and we must stop the pillage or perish. If we are consciously to control our flight through history, what we call management must become something new. If it does not, it merely gives us the illusion of control and it is an incidental appurtenance to so many helpless, tumbling lives.

To understand better the place of deliberate management, the self-conscious arrangement and use of institutions, within the larger natural scheme of things, I have included some comments on evolution, biology and ecology. At several points, I have also taken to unashamed analogizing between human and nonhuman systems. I am willing to put up with the censure this brings if it helps, in its small way, to topple man from his pedestal of conceit. I share the belief of many biologists that human conceit grossly distorts our understanding of ourselves and, in an age such as we live in, imperils our survival.

I would acknowledge the claim of many social scientists that man is a unique animal. This is clear enough in at least two respects: no other animal is as arrogant or as dangerous. But it is scarcely surprising that social science should have had difficulty seeing man in proper ecological perspective or that announcements such as "Man is the measure of all things," or "The proper study of man is man," would come easily to us. One is reminded of Mark Twain's rejoinder to the preacher who assured him that "man is the noblest work of God!" Twain's response was to ask, "Now, who found that out?" Social science is probably the last redoubt of this kind of self-deception, for, while it studies humankind's problems with commendable zeal, it does not enjoy looking at man as one among thousands of creatures, an organism that is, for all its grandiloquent posturing, a rather pathetic and helpless being. With a few happy exceptions, social scientists have not been willing to take physical and biological factors sufficiently into account in the study of human culture. As a result, they have produced curiously disembodied interpretations of social systems that fail to grasp the degree to which man, no less than leafmold and toads, grows from the loam and tilth of his planet.

In search for help in what is basically a problem of synthesis, I have been attracted to, indeed forced toward, systems theory. There is nothing mysterious about systems theory. It is essentially a point of view, an emphasis on the dynamic, interrelated, moving quality in the relationship of parts within wholes. General systems theory, a broader and more comprehensive philosophic posture, places special emphasis on the search for analogies and isomorphic relations, relations in structure such as exist between a musical score and its performance, or, in turn, the relationship between sounds from our hi-fi speakers and our aural processes. Systems theory has been an especially effective method of analyzing the complex cycles of reactions that occur in systems as varied as the human body and the economy. It has proved a potent tool in the hands of the physiologist and ecologist as well, and has, in fact, permeated virtually every aspect of modern thinking.

I find systems theory, as well as general systems theory, attractive because it puts our minds to thinking about codependent relations, the circuits and loops that tie systems into their environment. It may lead—I am sure it often does—to oversimplifications. But it also puts a bur under the seat of parochial thinkers and makes the business of straight-faced academic analysis less oppressively priggish. There is nothing, after all, quite so annoying as the intellectual prig who points out with studied daring that system analogies between, say, Londoners and slime mold can be overdrawn. This sort of observation may be reassuring to Londoners, but it is scarcely at issue in systems theory. Indeed, it is always easy to say things are complex. But if there is one thing more serious than the naïve fellow who unwittingly makes problems too simple, it is the learned fellow who deliberately makes them too complex. The value of a systems outlook is that it generates a distaste for static category-building, an impatience with logic-chopping and a certain useful boredom with ponderous exercises in taxonomy.

For aid in examining some of the epistemological and moral problems which mark the present predicament of our culture, I have turned to the work of C. S. Peirce. I find his writing attractive because he was so relentless in his efforts to say things clearly. He did not always succeed, but he did much of the time. I have tried to suggest that his beliefs about reality and his "doctrine of chances" are consistent with what we know about the evolution of the life process. I have tried to use his ideas to suggest where the foundation of a new altruism might be found, a moral order that man must now self-consciously embrace if he is to avoid extinction by his own hand. This sort of analysis has drawn me into philosophy more deeply than I would have preferred. But philosophy is, like war, too important to be left to professionals.

I have placed my interpretation of personality and social role into a systems framework, interpreting roles as devices for storing information that acts as a flywheel in social relations. On the other hand, to account for the mutant responses that must be available for any adaptive process to work, I have examined the creative personality, messianic acts and voluntarism, qualities of the Great Man. For ideas on the uses of deviance, I have turned to the literature on cultural revitalization. I have also studied such critics of romanticism as Geoffrey Scott, Irving Babbitt and T. E. Hulme. Their ideas help remove some of the humbug and ooze from our notion of the creative personality. Being creative is not a question, as some would have it, of possessing an eccentricity, an itchy beard and a beautiful soul. It is a question of whether or not a given inventive act proves valid in light of the requirements that govern evolution and survival, requirements that apply to the individual and the collective alike. This holds, I would insist, as much for the creation of the mosaics at Ravenna and the construction of La Grande Jatte as it does for the design of a conch shell or chambers of a termite community. Creation is a function of life. It could not be otherwise; the laws of life will not have it otherwise.

The problems of stereotypic response in animals and man, psychological set, social dogma and ideological pigheadedness, are closely linked to the problem of adaptive change. So I have also taken some time to look at the behavior of the professional in this respect, largely because his counsel is now so critical to what happens in the affairs of present world culture. The subject is broad, the literature large, and I have only touched on it selectively. My emphasis is essentially ecological. But a full-fledged analysis along these lines would require exhaustive experimental work. A study, for example, of the host-parasite relationship between various professionals and their clients, or between intellectuals and their converts, would probably pay rich dividends of social scientific insight. This entire topic, of course, is painfully personal to the academic, and naturally this tends to dampen enthusiasm for its exploration.

Even though ours is an era in which violence and affect seem to dominate life on an unprecedented world scale, I believe that the rationalization of group life, its arrangement in managed organizations, whether it be in General Motors or the Chinese Red Army, is a critical indicator of the magnitude of the problems of present-day world culture. But much of what we consider management is an illusion, and great global processes of natural governance are also at work. Furthermore, what management is real, and not illusory, comes to focus on acts of leadership, those vital conscious switch-point decisions that decide the course of human events.

There is a large and growing body of formal research literature on decision-making. But much of what goes on in the field is a callow professional parody of the real world of life and death, war and peace, conjugal strife and conjugal bliss. For truly penetrating studies of the moral issues involved in decision-making, one must turn to such thinkers as Kierkegaard, Dostoevsky, Jaspers and Buber. In their work, one catches sight of the actual nature of those critical non-programmed decisions that make life in modern times the compellingly individual thing that it is. Hence, again, my interest in messianic behavior. To my mind, the tendency in social science to avoid study of the Great Man, or at least to play him down in favor of collective processes—especially if his political views are not in fashion—is comparable to trying to build a science of neurophysiology while ignoring properties of the synapse.

Despite the fact that there are numerous books on industrial psychology and sociology, some of which are very thoughtful, and written by authors better equipped and more inclined to write them than I am, few attempt to place the study of managed organization within a larger theory of cultural change. The reason may be simply habit and professional proclivity. There is a truly enormous literature on administration, for instance, whose leitmotif seems to be the unrepentant platitude. Where discussion rises above the platitude, on the other hand, it is often lost in a Sargasso Sea of pedantry. To snatch a lively idea from this vast tangle of obfuscation, one must be both quick of hand and tireless. Some of my friends have devoted careers to this effort. I can only stand in awe of their devotion to so fatiguing an effort. The writers on bureaucracy determined to find out what Max Weber thought, for instance, are themselves a remarkable breed. Some have resolutely produced the most jejune and joyless body of writing thus far to issue from the hand of man. Still, I suppose its appreciation is an acquired taste, like that for olives. But one gets the uneasy feeling that many followers of Weber have not only taken to the olive, but have become convinced that there is a secret savor yet hidden somewhere in the leached pit.

Regardless of this somewhat glum view of what passes for the theory of management, and at the risk of seeming to enjoy inconsistency, I have tried to indicate at several points why modern managerial thought is failing us, both as a science and as an art, and what radical reforms are required in it if it is to help us survive. I believe that in many respects radical departure from orthodox views is necessary and perhaps imminent. But I would stress that change and progress should not be confused. In our culture they often are.

I have felt little compulsion to add intentionally to the literature on bureaucracy as such. I personally have lived the life of an administrator long enough to realize how dull it can be—or, at least, how chimerical its joys can be—yet, also, how addicting it is. I know the long halls and conspiratorial crannies of bureaucracy, and have perspired helping to hold part of a bureaucracy together. So I have made a few remarks about rite and ritual in managed organizations. They will be of interest, perhaps, to that occasional manager who refuses to surrender his vitality to the sallow indecision that surrounds him daily, corroding will and making mice of men. But the primary intention of this book is to indicate what is happening to the idea of progress and what the future may be as the collapse of the progress culture becomes evident to all of us.

The Death
of Progress

———————

I

OUR TIGHTENING
PREDICAMENT

I WILL BEGIN by noting what is obvious. Awesome cultural
change has overtaken the present era. There is a sense of
desperation in the air, a sense that change is sweeping everything before it, a sense that man has been pitchforked by science and technology into a new and precarious age, that the
human race itself has lost its direction. Under the merciless
glare of empiricism, venerable religious values have decom-
posed before our very eyes. Once-revered political beliefs no
longer seem self-evident truths. Revolutionary ideologies exert
violent torque upon democratic institutions; nihilistic mobs
careen down the boulevards of our cities.

By any measure, this is a remarkable time in which we live.
On the one hand, it is a hyperrational period. Science and
technology have laid claim to possessions that once belonged
only to God. We place men on planets, rearrange the genetic
disposition of plants and animals, transplant organs from one
man to another and from beast to man. Soon we will slow,
perhaps even reverse, the process of aging. But it is also an
antirational time. Urban violence swells, pointless perversities
invade the arts, the young are caught up in a new romanticism
of the most viscid kind. The hyperrational and the antirational

seem to have been sworn to each other in a devilish secret marriage, an illicit perfervid pact. "A battle arises," says Jaspers, "for and against reason. Opposed to pure, transparent reason's drive toward rest within the conceivable, stands a drive to destroy reason, not only to indicate its limits, but to enslave it." [1]

The course of change in the modern progress culture, in simplest terms, is this. The religious, political and economic forms that rose in the West during the age of faith gave way steadily in the post-Renaissance world to the forces of social rationalization, science, technology and to the conviction that man's life on earth could be steadily and deliberately perfected. As a result, the old unexamined habits and attitudes, the habits and attitudes that had the cohesive strength of tradition within them, were destroyed. Wholesale rationalization of experience has not only left the past broken and in ruin; it has also left everything in doubt. It thereby generated a new level of collective consciousness. Everything was questioned and it soon replaced our older beliefs with new definitions of reality. We arrived at a point where substance, solid things themselves, seemed to dissolve into a translucent world of abstract inferences. The new reality is constructed with the machinery of science and technology, from the data of spectrographs, oscilloscopes, radiotelescopes, encephalographs, a vast and tenuous web of deductions held together by ever more labyrinthian mathematics.

Hovering above it all, waiting to settle like a silent predator upon the remnants of flesh-and-blood experience, was the gray and implacable criterion of efficiency. It soon insinuated itself into every crib and crevice of modern life. The stealth and power with which it intruded upon tradition became obvious wherever the progress culture met an old established way. It consumed every traditional belief in its path and customs were

4

reduced to ash. It now seems to be driving everything before it, economic, political and religious beliefs, primitive peoples, traditional societies, masses of poor, masses of men of every kind. In the progress culture, survival seems to depend upon constant, conscious calculations, cost-benefit ratios, costs per kilowatt-hour, costs of building, costs of living, costs of destroying.

But hyperrationalism does not add meaning to our lives; it generates doubt. It generates questions faster than it can supply answers, and as Ludwig Wittgenstein reminded us, "Doubt can only exist where there is a question." [2] So in this abstract world bleached white by the demands of hyperrationality, we scurry from one desperate refuge to another, like lizards seeking respite from a desert sun. First, we fixate on creature comforts, as if Gross National Product could tell us the meaning of it all. Then, we sink ourselves in compulsive hedonism, trying to force the secrets of our existence from the juice and prurience of our basest impulses. Or we shrink into soporific pietism, or try to escape into nostalgia, narcotics, rural communes or mumbled excerpts from Eastern philosophies severed from their Eastern cultures. We try frantically to pretend that mortality is not what science has made it out to be.

But, alas, we cannot invent meaning as if it were a plastic to be concocted in a vat. In a world such as we live in today, a world in which ancient values lie in decay all about us, totems of convictions to which we refuse any longer to attend, science becomes a hyperrational lust for certitude and our desperation merely becomes efficient madness. Hyperrationalism goads us toward a will to believe, a will to embrace anything that might substitute for the dead certainties of the past. We are driven toward a fierce new romantic voluntarism, weird and various regressive political beliefs, demands for participative madness, direct action, hangings in the public square, blood. We join stampeding mobs shouting antinomies —"It is forbidden to forbid!"—or hurl obscenities toward a heaven that contains no God. If we are men of science, we may commit ourselves to a new romantic "pursuit of truth," without care or compass, and we vent the same enthusiasm on development of anthrax sprays to kill whole cities—there are, after all, truths to be learned there, too—as we do on increasing the yield of sorghum. But we do not survive in order to think, we think in order to survive; and that inversion is the root of our quandary.

Jung accounts in part for our present predicament by his law of psychic compensation. It says that "for every piece of conscious life that loses its importance and value . . . there arises a compensation in the unconscious." [3] Jung used this law to explain contradictions in such cultures as Germany's: how a people of such remarkable scientific accomplishment could be buried for over a decade under the hissing magma of Nazi madness; how brilliant and creative nations are swept by epidemics of desperate and degenerate violence.

But Jung's law is only half the law we need, since we must account in the first place for the rise of collective consciousness itself. I will argue here that such consciousness is born in the ruins of social habit, that it represents doubt. Jung's law, in other words, must also be read in reverse. For every piece of unconscious cultural life that loses its importance and value, there arises compensatory consciousness. When we link the two together, as halves of a larger law, we have a principle that describes the shift of meaning from nonconscious traditional values to rational and then hyperrational values, and, in turn, the further shift toward new forms of nonconscious action. This is what has taken place in the West since classic times as Western culture's mass of knowledge grew, molted,

6

decayed and yet thrived again. And so the breakdown of traditions was accompanied by the rise of compensatory consciousness. This new consciousness first manifested itself in the Renaissance and the Enlightenment. But it then became annealed with science and technology and the concern for efficiency. It showed itself in histories such as Oswald Spengler's, modern art and the revolutionary ideas of politically conscious masses. But we cannot sustain the load of such consciousness for long, and we are now beginning to buckle under its demands. The requirements of abstract existence are too great and men seek to escape them by turning again toward crepuscular myths, antirationalism, the pleasurable numbness of sensate values, and so we descend to a semi-conscious cultural state.

If one ponders the matter, there is a striking antithetical quality about two sets of values, beliefs and traits now prominent in our culture. I list them below. I do not wish to suggest that they are precisely paired, or even commensurable as sociological categories. But set alongside one another they make it clear that there has been a lurch in our world view toward those actions, habits and beliefs that I have listed under affective responses. I list the first under the hyperrational because I do not want to confuse aspects of them with what we ordinarily think of as rational or enlightened. The hyper-rational is more obsessive, more presumptuous, more often a caricature of reason than its epitome. The other I call affective because it is more a matter of feeling than of thought. I do not believe that the shift is necessarily good or desirable, only that it is a powerful force within historical circumstances. Unfortunate though it may be, the hyperrational has left modern man stranded, and meaning will return to his life more through his senses than his intellect. But consider the following two sets of traits as cultural change indicators:

hyperrationality in science and technology	affect in the counter-culture
the desire for long-range social planning	"now" values
belief in the causal principle	voluntarism
over-emphasis on due process	demands for direct action
cerebral existentialism	pop religions
growth economics	subversive science
the progress ideology	a steady-state ideology

The scientific and technological view of life places high—indeed, central—value upon reason, prediction, order and conscious control; it requires looking ahead, planning; it projects model societies, Marxist paradises and B. F. Skinner's *Walden Two*. On its surface lies the causal principle, but beneath it now is a curious cerebral fixation on abstractions, forced connections between events, between momentary precedent and consequence. There is often an aura of conceit about it, too, as in science, where humility is frequently skin deep and fashion dictates that one couch whatever one says in endless courtly caveats. The other set of habits and beliefs, those I list on the right, are essentially antirational and nonrational. It lauds emotion, spontaneity and unpredictability to the point that trying to have no habits becomes an absurd habit. It disdains conscious order and often revels in disorder. It represents a two-dimensional "now" world. It is noncerebral, full of unspoken intensity, commitments to volition, to "direct" action, to freedom "now." It replaces the abstract world of causation and correlation with pop religions, youth cultism, "happenings," astrology and the *I Ching*. It is short-tempered and resentful before the slow, tedious and bloodless constructions of "due process." It rejects anything that would bleed will of energy, or mock the mystical with proofs.

The shift toward the affective is a deep, pervasive thing, now

8

taking place at the very foundation of the hyperrational. Thus respected journals like *Science* begin to publish oddly contrived papers such as "Sensuous-Intellectual Complementarity in Science: Countercultural Epistemology Has Something to Contribute to the Science of Complex Systems." [4] Ecology emerges as a "subversive" force in the progress culture, an indictment of the economics of gluttony.[5] And now we see the idea of endless technological progress subjected to the irony of computer test, and the results are published in a disturbing book called *The Limits to Growth*.[6]

The present institutional turmoil around the world is perhaps a temporary thing, and just as a hurricane howls itself out as it grinds against the earth, the present fury of change may howl itself out. A new world will then take shape. It may be a new order as rationally relentless and unsparing as anything we have yet imagined. It may be the more remorseless simply because we may have learned rationally to take the nonrational into account. It may also produce a new élite, an era ruled by philosopher kings, or megalomaniacs, or possibly only simple-minded brutes ministered by computers. Most probably it will show itself as a wholly natural thing, perhaps a new religiosity, a merger of science and mysticism. Signs of such a merger are already all about us. Regardless of the specific course these events foreshadow, for us to survive we must certainly build our culture on a truer view of man's place in nature than was so in the progress culture.

Spengler said in 1922, in his preface to the revised edition of *The Decline of the West,* that pessimistic though it seems, modern history was inevitably a philosophy of destiny and, in the case of the Western historian, the self-conscious study of the latter days of our Western culture. I believe he was correct, and in that sense this book may be but a footnote to his monumental study. But the progress culture is caught in

9

a dilemma peculiar to modern times, not unlike that forced upon us in physics by the Heisenberg uncertainty principle. The velocity of events around us makes it nearly impossible to judge our position within their flow, and almost anything we conclude about where we stand in history seems at once naïve and futile. But the special difficulty today is to understand what is happening to us as our self-consciousness declines, as we enter an era of affect and a collective retreat from consciousness takes place. It is especially painful to consider what this retreat may mean for freedom and civility. In a nonconscious era, half-conscious men will be kings.

We may be caught in a great cycle of cultural change rather than the final period of the decay of our Western world. This is a possibility. The problem then becomes one of trying to determine whether present circumstances are preconditions to cultural revitalization. I would like to believe this is so but the evidence is not convincing. If it is so, the gloom that I find pressing in upon us may be a prelude to something better, progress of its own sort. And some readers will say that I am simply playing on the term "progress" as I use it in this analysis. I do not think this is so, for surely the traditional idea of progress is more than belief in inevitable change, and it has had an incredible effect upon us. The same brain that once believed that man's place in nature was relatively fixed, and that social systems are not to be tampered with carelessly, has become the site of powerful amplifier beliefs about our use of the world. Progress seems to have become a lethal *idée fixe,* irreversibly destroying the very planet it depends upon to survive. The progress culture is the first high technological culture whose basic values act as a great complex of positive feedback forces, a consideration of no small significance. Such positive feedback processes, as I shall indicate in more detail later, are self-amplifying, like a fire burning out of control. The higher its heat, the greater its lust for fuel; and the more fuel it consumes, the higher its heat rises, until it exhausts what it depends upon.

The crisis building about us, I shall argue, is the sort of cultural circumstance that unleashes social mutation, personified in the Great Man. I will therefore examine his visions, half-mad insights and creative drive. For it seems likely that as the world predicament of the progress culture worsens we will turn increasingly toward Great Man solutions. I can only speculate upon what a new order may be like, who may rule it, what philosophy may inform it, what beliefs may turn it toward decent ends, what may bring it to an end.

Our present world tells us little about all of this. The past no longer stands at our elbow to guide our steps. We are at once free of the past and in dire need of a reliable substitute. We are being forced, as Jung put it, to "resort to decisions." [7] Yet Jung's phrase does not tell us what happens when our decisions let us down. For nature, too, is making decisions and whether we attempt to engineer our destiny or not, uncompromising natural forces are exerting themselves as powerful, spontaneous correctives upon the progress culture. Their impact frequently leaves us shocked and dismayed. We feel a sense of betrayal too, for this is not what we had expected when science and technology promised to build a shining new world for us. Certainly it is clear that the troubles of our world are driving us toward surrender of many preconceptions with which our belief in the inevitability of progress once sustained us.

II

THE IDEA
OF PROGRESS
AS A STRATEGY

I WOULD STRESS HERE early in my argument that this volume
is not a study in the intellectual history of the belief in
progress. There is a rich literature of that kind and little
need for me to attempt to add my bit to it. There are books
such as J. B. Bury's *The Idea of Progress,* Georges Sorel's
The Illusions of Progress and hundreds of essays on the subject such as that in *An Intellectual and Cultural History of
the Western World,* by Harry Elmer Barnes. The roots of the
idea are many and old. One goes to the fifth-century Pelagian
heresy that denied original sin; another is the writing of the
fourteenth-century Muslim scholar Ibn-Khaldun. The idea of
progress also drew upon the excitement and free booty of the
great age of exploration during which the bounds of the
Western world seemed almost to explode. But by the eigh-
teenth century the idea was everywhere in the air of Western
culture, and such men as Giovanni Vico, Anne Robert Jacques
Turgot, the Marquis de Condorcet and Auguste Comte all
devoted their pens to the mystery of the forces that made for
the inexorable improvement of the human condition. To Count
Claude Henri de Saint-Simon, the golden age was not behind

us in some Classic Elysium, but before us. Our fathers had not seen it, nor would we, but our children would. It was therefore essential that we "clear the way for them." [1] During the nineteenth century, the idea spread and took firm hold of the popular mind and new scientific discoveries only added to the conviction that man was the elect vehicle for a grand march toward paradise on earth. Both capitalist and communist societies now share these beliefs and in that sense we must think of them as a single culture. The planet was something to be "developed"; frontiers existed that they might be "rolled back." Massive material, as well as ideological forces, were unleashed by the industrial revolution and steam power as well as socialism fed into the stream of social change. During the nineteenth century, scientific discoveries followed one upon another, and such as that of Charles Darwin had particularly powerful impact. They all added conviction to the assumption that material and social advancement was a veritable law of life. By the turn of the present century, the idea had taken profound hold on the Western imagination.

In America in particular, where a vast continent lay open, vacant but for a few savages unblessed by the knowledge of what progress held in store for them, it seemed only logical that progress would work its ultimate miracles of transformation. But it did not. The dream was stalked by chimeras: "hide men" slaughtering bison in such numbers that putrescent carcasses covered mile upon mile of prairie land on the Little Missouri; the burial of the Sioux slaughtered at Wounded Knee, stripped by souvenir hunters and tumbled, naked and frozen, into a pit, on New Year's Day, 1891; factories with iron hearts in which children worked sixteen hours a day; cities layered with soot; rivers polluted enough to be flammable; "Fat Man," ten feet eight inches tall and obese with evil, exploding over Nagasaki; Hanna Coal Company's "Gem of Egypt," with its shovel that has a bite of 200 tons, making its contribution to the 71,000 square miles of America that will be strip-mined by 1980; filthy air, filthy water and boastful people; dying eagles and Las Vegas billboards.

The mere suggestion that what we call progress could slow, and even end, is still greeted by most people in our society as a preposterous heresy—or at least something we need not worry about in the foreseeable future—and our national policy is still shaped by progress ideologists. They continue, in the face of the starkest kind of evidence, to descant on the "growth of our GNP," bigger and more of everything. But such technologies as that of taconite mining, shale oil extraction and recycling make it abundantly clear that traditional pillage economics is about to be replaced by scavenger economics. This will be a demeaning experience for such an energetic and optimistic culture as ours. But there are fundamental laws of energy and resource use at work beneath these events, and no amount of technological wizardry is going to reverse the trend. A high irony of the American predicament is that the managerial arts and sciences that sustained the progress culture were led by the United States. Our leadership hastened our agonizing confrontation with what "progress" really means, and we are being forced well ahead of most other nations to face the issue.

TRUTH-USE

To understand what the idea of progress has meant to modern man, we must realize that all living systems, from the simplest single-celled organism to a complex culture, are strategies by which life contests with the uncertain universe about it. I want, therefore, to place the idea of progress against the background of natural events and to ask several basic questions about what we know of our universe and what this means regarding how our idea of progress helps or hinders us in the struggle to survive. We must step back briefly and examine some of the old persistent questions of philosophy.

In one literary version of the arrest of Jesus by Pontius Pilate, the Lord responds to the question "What is truth?" with another question, "What is reality?" This may be an artistic liberty, since I do not find such a reply recorded in the Gospels. On the other hand, it is a profound response that cuts to the heart of epistemology. The question and response stand out in particularly high relief if we consider them alongside the ideas of Charles S. Peirce, the founder of pragmatism, a brilliant man whose thought later took a strange and disturbing turn when William James and John Dewey set to elaborating on it. I need not say more here than to note that most critics of pragmatism have not really come to grips with its founder's ideas but have been distracted by James's and Dewey's distortions of what Peirce said. Peirce was, of course, well aware of what was being done to his pioneering philosophic studies, especially at the hands of James, and he suggested at one point that his philosophy be retitled "pragmaticism," a name "ugly enough to be safe from kidnappers." [2]

A fundamental idea in Peirce's thinking is that the "real" is separate from what we believe about it. It is "that whose characters are independent of what anybody may think them to be." [3] It is independent, however, "not necessarily of thought in general, but only of what you or I or any finite number of men may think about it. . . ." Objectivity is shared subjectivity, inevitably a public thing. We cannot, then, simply assume that reality is what each of us makes it or that what is true for you may not be true for me. The "real" is indubitably "out there," separate from what the individual may believe about it. Wishes, prejudices, dreams are not enough. Despite the fact that a degree of subjective malleability surrounds that unbudging thing outside us, it remains, as C. I. Lewis has said, "hard, independent and unalterable to our will." [4]

Once given the notion that the real and what we think about it are distinct, a theory of meaning follows that says that what gives an opinion its utility is the degree to which it corresponds to reality. Use implies, or supplies, a context for the idea, and that context is the consequences that flow from it. Peirce summed the point up by saying that the tenet "By their fruits ye shall know them" is the basic test of any idea's value. So the meaning of an idea or opinion, or habit—which is an idea routinized in us—depends upon the match between it and actuality, in its verification by use. The weight we can put on an idea, an opinion, varies as a result with the number of tests to which it is exposed. Or, as Hans Reichenbach put it, "Weight is what a degree of probability becomes if it is applied to a single case." [5] Therefore, absolute truth, full weight, would be the same as an errorless prediction. We cannot arrive at such a condition, though we do approach it asymptomatically the more we expose an idea to use and verify it. But since any idea can be overturned by further investigation, weight is always related to the frequency of tests.

Whether or not we substitute the words "belief," "theory," "opinion" or "habit" for the term "idea" does not affect the basic point of Peirce's view. Nor does it matter whether we consider the idea or opinion to be learned or non-learned, an individual or a collective thing. Meaning lies in use. It is an active, transactional thing. The meaning of an idea, like the value of a pair of pliers, depends on how well it helps us grip reality. We may speak then of the meaning of opinions, ideas, beliefs and habits as their truth-use. The same may be said of grunts, imprecations or exhortations. But I would go further, to an opposite extreme perhaps, and include the thing we call "culture." Because the ideas that compose them have varying weight, cultures, too, can be said to have relative truth-use.

I realize that my short résumé of some of Peirce's thought may be crude and that it blurs such distinctions as made by the analytic school of philosophers between cognitive, emotive and instigative uses of language. My purpose is not to rob the reader of the pleasure of puzzling over these fastidious distinctions but merely to suggest that there is really no such thing as a totally unused idea. An idea comes into being as a use. We can, of course, hold an idea at the ready, as we may in deferring action based upon it. But this does not mean it has no consequences in the meantime. They may be minor, or entirely latent, but unless an idea is ultimately used in some sense or other, it is meaningless and as an idea does not really exist. One can toy with the idea of what is latent and what is forever dead, but the only thing I wish to underscore is the active, dynamic nature of ideas, both those held by individuals and those held collectively by groups. The opportunity that opinions provide for disputatious games among thinkers is actually a minor bonus given us when ideas are born. The sport they provide comes from the fact that even the most esoteric and preciously irrelevant idea is born with some of its use already attached. Every idea, be it as trivial or subtle as a daydream or as critical to life and death as a battle map, has, then, a given weight at a given time.

What this implies for the progress ideology may be more obvious if we see communities as Norton Long, the political scientist, has described them, as "ecologies of games." [6] It is a good phrase since it suggests that the rules of such a game are constantly being put to test, one against the other and all against the environment. Each is a bet against uncertainty.

Every organism and every culture, in other words, is a strategy and its truth-use determines which shall and which shall not survive. The progress ideology is part of the natural order of living strategies, and like those of the neurotic or the honest man—assuming they can be distinguished to some degree at least—it works poorly or well for the short or long term depending on its match with reality. We must now look at the way cultures govern themselves as strategies and what in fact a strategy is.

THE ANATOMY OF STRATEGIES

Von Moltke the Elder said at one point that a "strategy" was "nothing but a sequence of *ad hoc* expedients." [7] In a sense, then, the great general was English in his point of view, since the muddling-through strategy has always been something of a point of pride among the English. They used it extensively, both to build and to dismantle a world empire. But the genius of the English in all of this was their intuitive realization that in the affairs of men more is decided by accident and ineptitude than by intention. Although muddling through is rarely dignified by calling it a strategy, it does in fact represent a short-run strategy and its truth-use derives from its flexibility. Its structure has been described with baroque academic elegance as "successive limited comparisons." [8]

Regardless of the merits of muddling through, the concept of a strategy deserves a close look. But we need a more serviceable definition than Von Moltke's. Herbert Simon has given us a less haughty definition than the German's, certainly a more solemn one. He calls a strategy a "detailed prescription, or program, that governs the sequence of responses of a system to a complex task environment." [9]

There are two obvious components in both Von Moltke's and Simon's definitions of strategy. An external reality or task-environment is posited which makes the strategy necessary in the first place, a reality that generates an opinion about it. There is also a sequence of acts linked together to form the strategy. The strategy is a dynamic thing with an internal tactical form. The truth-use of the strategy will be determined by the match it makes with reality, and it is this match that provides the basis for its predictive power.

The matching capacity of a strategy implies that there is an isomorphic relationship, a structural correspondence of some kind, between it and the problem. If it is to be useful, the tactical logic inherent to it will reflect structural features of the task. The shape of an ordinary flat-head screwdriver, for example, betrays the shape of the screwhead it is meant to match, and if we meet a Phillips screwhead with such a screwdriver it will be almost useless. In the same way, a healthy personality will fit the minimum requirements of the society in which the individual must function. The so-called cultural shock that some people experience when they move to a strange part of the world is comparable to confronting a screw with the wrong kind of screwdriver.

On a large collective scale, cultures, too, must meet strategic requirements and their technologies are often marvels of tactical match between a task and its solution. Perhaps there are no better illustrations of such solutions than those of the Eskimo. He invented snow goggles made of wood, ivory or bone, with a narrow slit for each eye, to prevent snow blindness, and designed his kayak so that he could lace himself into a watertight hatch. But his most dramatic "sequence of responses to a task environment" may be the use of the kayak in heavy seas:

> As the sea curls down over them they voluntarily capsize, receive it on the bottom of the kayak, and when it has passed right themselves again.[10]

The predictive strength of a strategy is measured, like the truth-use of an opinion, by the rules of inference and probability. "All predictors," as Arnold Tustin put it, "are essentially analogues of the external situation." [11] Any strategy, in other words, whether it is a sequence of responses in use of a hand tool or a sequence of responses by a culture, stands or falls on how well it predicts events about it. Like a gambler, it lives by the success of its inductions; it thrives or dies on how well it reads reality. The progress ideology, I shall argue, is proving a poor analogue of the "external situation."

The tactical logic inherent to a strategy can be identified in simple problem-solving behavior. When we must find the proper key on our key chain to open a door in the dark, we may try all keys of a certain size or shape, or we may move around the chain clockwise using one key at a time, or we may simply resort to random trial and error in the hope that chance will turn the trick. In more complex strategies, the internal tactical structure may be enormously complicated. When medical researchers face an infectious organism and must match it with an undiscovered antibiotic, or when military authorities must develop a retaliatory strike capacity for an enemy whose strength can only be guessed, whole stables of mathematicians and computers may be needed to try to arrange a set of tactics. Or, when a society is faced with such difficulties as we now face—populations growing out of control, cities crumbling for want of sufficient finance, an avalanche of welfare, drug and public health problems—it may attempt, as we are now clumsily attempting, to invent forms of social engineering in which armies of planners and technicians endeavor to reform the "establishment" by bringing to bear new hyperrational tactics. The problem, nonetheless, is the same in each case, the need to establish problem-solving devices which are valid analogues of the external situation.

The rate of change in the task-environment, as I have already suggested, affects the degree of match which a given strategy is able to maintain with its problems—a simple enough point, but one that is also worth examining more closely. An ordinary wrench head, for example, is a fixed strategy that is designed to match nuts and bolts of given sizes and shapes, a stable task. In a world where nuts and bolts are constant in size and shape, such a wrench is obviously preferable to a more flexible but complex device such as a monkey wrench. But such fixed strategies always face a degree of uncertainty— a stripped bolthead, for instance, or boltheads that have been swollen by heat. The superiority of an adjustable wrench to an ordinary wrench lies in its flexibility as a predictor. It is a dynamic strategy, an analogue of a mixed bag of nuts and bolts. Its costs, on the other hand, are higher than that of a simpler tool. It is more complicated to make and maintain and it requires continuous adjustment. Its use involves a series of tactics, a spiral of actions and reactions, changing as the external situation requires.

Whatever form a strategy may take, it is basically a design, then, for a controlled series of responses to a problem, a method of reducing error in solving problems. Its features can be identified in greater detail by looking at cybernetic systems. They were first described systematically by W. Ross Ashby, Norbert Wiener and others during the early nineteen-forties.[12] Since that time, the cybernetic literature has become vast and highly technical. It is basic to the sciences of electrical engineering, neurophysiology and many complex biological systems. We should note that cyberneticists do not say that living systems are mere machines. As one authority put it, "All we know at present is that brains are less like levers and gears than like radar and thermostats." [13] Cybernetic principles have also made substantial contributions to economics and political science. They are implicit in Keynesian economics and in work of political scientists such as Karl Deutsch.[14]

A common illustration of a self-regulating system is the ordinary thermostatically controlled furnace. The desired temperature setting is matched with the actual temperature of the room, and by a simple system in which expanding and contracting strips of metal act as an on and off switch, the furnace is told what to do. Our own bodies operate, though in an infinitely more complex system of messages, loops and triggers, in a similar way, so that a continuous series of stimulus-response-stimulus signals circulates through us.*

Such systems are called negative feedback systems, because information fed back concerning past performance is used to oppose what the system is already doing. Since the flow of error information permits continuous monitoring of match to the problem, error is necessary to the operation of any such system. It should be noted here that learning in a biological system is related to its capacity to register error. This may explain why imitative learning in animals is more rapid when the demonstrator errs than when it makes a correct response.[15] Which also brings to mind the observation made by Liddell Hart that in war generals learn more from disasters than from their victories.

---

* Cybernetic models for living systems have been described by many investigators. One of the clearest models is that of Powers, Clark and McFarland. Their model has five variables arranged as several functions. Its details need not concern us here, but its essentials are input, the relationship between environmental variables and feedback; a comparator function, the relationship between feedback and the system's standards, what the authors call a "reference signal" (the system's error is the difference between performance and standard); and an output function, the relationship of error and output on each cycle of action. The input-comparator-output relationship could be called a "strategy." (W. T. Powers, R. K. Clark and R. I. McFarland, "A General Feedback Theory of Human Behavior," *Perceptual and Motor Skills,* Monograph Supplement I–VII [1960].)

Insofar as a negative feedback system tries to reduce the difference between standards and performance, intention and behavior, the "ought" and the "is"—values and facts, if you like—it not only acts in a convergent way, but is also purposive.[16] Purposive behavior has been defined in both mechanical and neural systems as negative feedback processes in which goals alter behavior after the system has begun to move toward its goal.* The "will" of a purposive act, then, is the energy we are able to exert to reduce error toward zero to reach our goals.

Relatively unchanging values of the traditional sort have negative feedback effects. There are many illustrations from anthropology. The primitives of Australia, for instance, often defined the ideal life in terms of a sacred, mythic past peopled by ancestral beings and culture heroes. What was not found in this mythic past was inadmissible to the present. Thus one such people, the Yir Yoront, rejected introduction of the canoe from a neighboring people on the ground that it was not part of the ancient, mythic ideal.[17] In traditional societies, their values often had the same effect; e.g., the Classic belief in Fate or the Christian concept of man's natural culpability and fall from grace. They tend to push deviate behavior toward a norm that changes very slowly if at all. Cynicism and resignation can do the same thing. Diogenes believed that "the privilege of the gods is to want nothing, and of those like the gods to want but little." [18] Tchekov has one of his characters, the Siberian exile Simeon, assert that "if you want to be happy you must want nothing." [19]

This represents the very antithesis of the progress ideology, which is a positive feedback system of ideas whose critical characteristic is its capacity to amplify itself. We in

* Such goal settings should not be confused with a future state of the system.

America seem to believe that the idea is the only natural one for man, that to be happy he must want everything. The progress ideology fixates on getting more, making more, using more; and so to quiet our anxieties about why we live we frantically gorge ourselves on materialism.

There are many ready illustrations of the positive feedback process. As I mentioned earlier, an ordinary fire is one. The higher the temperature rises, the faster the fuel is consumed; in turn, the faster the fuel is consumed, the higher the heat rises. Chain reactions and vicious circles represent such processes. Another illustration is that involving industrial production, sales and advertising. If part of the profits from sales is diverted to advertising to generate new demand—that is, to change the system's expectations—it generates higher levels of production, more profits, more advertising and still more demand, until the market is saturated or the firm runs out of resources.

Control of these positive feedback processes can be extremely difficult. They are literally explosive in nature. In many aspects, the so-called revolution of rising economic expectations among the lower economic classes around the world is a problem in positive feedback. From a systems point of view, riots and civil stress are like overheating in a machine or a fever in a mammal. Increasing speed of communication around the world has made economic differences increasingly obvious; the result has been an abrupt shift in the expectations of most societies, and it has increased social tensions, often triggering what Kenneth Boulding calls "spite revolutions," [20] outbursts in which a nation destroys its most resourceful people, like a hungry mob that expresses its desperation by burning the granary.

The belief in the perfectibility of life on earth, hitched to the discoveries of science and the achievements of technology, had similar effects. They tightened the hold of the progress ideology on modern culture to the point that stabilizing counterinfluences were overwhelmed. Social evolutionists came forward to insist that survival of the fittest justified child labor, market skulduggery and the coarsest of robber barons. Herbert Spencer argued that human perfection was not only possible but ultimately certain, and he opposed poor laws, state-supported education, housing regulation, tariffs, even public postal systems.[21] Other versions of this faith in the inevitable good that would result from the spontaneous forces of growth and evolution appeared in other settings. Many were contradictory in detail, but all believed that the universe at last was wide open and man was the great free adventurer within it. John Dewey attacked the claim that the structure of mind was fixed as a standpatter argument, and his theory of educational "growth" is suffused with the progress spirit.[22] There were also the George Babbitts, for whom hard work and a bit of good promotion would put all things right in the world. Anything we can do, we can do better, and every community must have its booster clubs.

The positive feedback characteristic of such views committed us to a course of development that in fact scored very impressive short-range improvements in the quality of life in the progress culture. But the price was long-run instability. Preoccupation with short-run gains, something that could be seen, something practical, lent an exaggerated sanctity to the idea of "efficiency," so that means became ends. Science and technology took on the sacred aura of an almost supernatural force, the weapons that would drive famine, disease and pestilence from the earth. Together these beliefs acted like a gigantic valve opener on the flow of energy through the progress culture, and a flood of effort followed, as did massive environmental change. But this change brings with it rising public anxiety and ends with the "twilight of the booster." Thus, confronted with the incompatibility between the economic appeal of a huge new airport and the quality of life in Newburgh, New York, the booster is torn by conflict.

It's not just anger, it's anguish. . . . A Trojan Horse has begun to disgorge its contents into his thinking, to undermine his optimism.[23]

Such doubt produces what systems theory calls "hunt" behavior, and it often results in overreaction, first in one direction and then in another, so that we now witness simultaneous concern for "the ecology" and violent attacks upon "environmentalists" for their gloomy view of things. But "hunt" develops because the error signal moving through a system reinforces rather than decreases overreaction.[24] A common illustration is the driver skidding out of control on an icy highway. Another is cerebellar tremor in which the victim's hands oscillate wildly when he reaches out to grasp an object. The same sort of oscillation plagues economic systems where boom-bust cycles may occur. Indeed, planning on a large scale is especially vulnerable to miscalculations that set such oscillation in motion. Hence, centralized organizations tend to make fewer but bigger errors than decentralized organizations.[25] Such was the problem that Eastern European planners faced several years ago when they legalized abortion as a birth control measure. As birth rates fell below what had been anticipated, the law was abruptly reversed, resulting in an avalanche of illegitimate births and a crisis in social welfare management.

We can engineer some stability into managed systems by using regulator loops similar to those found in biological or social systems. The numerous small internal damping processes of complex food webs, as compared with simpler food chains, prevent excessive oscillations in prey-predator relations;[26] and in some parts of Balinese culture social rules require that quarrels be "registered" before they can build up to a climactic showdown.[27] Control of excessive fluctuation is the reason, of course, for crop diversification, mixed financial investment and varied combinations of military hardware. On the other hand, what is gained in stability by diversification is often lost in speed and precision of response. Stability is always a question of change within the system relative to change outside it.

When the strategy of one system is the task environment of another, we have a game. Because the output of one may affect the reference signal of another, as well as its input, such relationships can become extremely complex. Body chemistry contains many such systems.[28] Nature in fact is a great tangle of interconnected strategies, a "sociology of nature," [29] some host-parasite relations, others symbiotic relations, and others forms of overt mutual aid.[30] Termites harbor intestinal protozoans that produce an enzyme that makes digestion of wood possible. Man, too, is locked into a system of complex co-dependent relations, with intestinal bacteria as well as with domesticated plants and animals. Each subpart in such a community is party to the ecological game, and the predictor value of each depends upon how well it mirrors the community of strategies within which it must live.

Interesting rules evolve to govern these relations. The noctuid moth, for example, has receptors that enable it to pick up the radar signals emitted by bats that prey on it. Receipt of a signal by the moth triggers a frantic erratic flight pattern that makes the moth a more difficult target.[31] The flight pattern randomizes success of the predator and regulates possibilities of an overkill of the moths and malnutrition among the bats.

Many human beliefs that we have put down as superstitions

27

have similar ecological functions. O. K. Moore has identified this in divination practices among the Naskapi Indians. The Naskapi direct their hunts by scapulimancy, a practice in which random cracks in burnt caribou blades are used as a guide for hunters. Moore says that the practice prevents formation of "detrimental habits," though he does not really specify what this means from a system point of view.[32] Evidently scapulimancy regulates the Naskapi-caribou ecological relationship in much the manner that the noctuid flight pattern regulates its relationship to bats. It prevents too much short-term success. The superstition probably came into being by accident, was selected out by social evolutionary tests and became embedded in custom as an ecological rule beneficial to both caribou and Naskapi.

Such phenomena are numerous in nature and it is only within recent decades that their significance has begun to be understood. Aggressive behavior, for example, can have a spacing or territorial function and, by distributing animals properly, assures use of environmental energy that assists a species in the struggle to survive.[33] But it is worth observing that aggression between species directs its attention to possibilities for enlarging its niche, while altruistic responses— such as the sacrifices of a mother to protect her young—help insure survival by strengthening rules of community cohesion within the species. Displacement of aggression toward objects different from those that elicit it apparently can then have a harmonic function, and by taxing individuality it binds groups into communities. Displacement can transpose selfish aggressive energy into altruistic energy, a centrifugal into a centripetal social force. But as the stuff of individuality is made collective, we reduce adaptive potential. A new and critical social problem is whether or not displacement behavior in large collectivities can be used toward altruistic ends without sacrificing the survival value of deviate, selfish response. Humans have been reasonably successful in developing strong rules for such conversion of selfish energy into group energy within the family, tribe and nation. Conversion of it beyond these reaches has been difficult. But this is largely what the issue of law, order and justice is about, both within nations and amongst them. Gaetano Mosca measured the level of civilization by its level of "juridical defense," its capacity to protect its members from their own predatory impulses.[34] Walter Lippmann measures a civilization's level of good by its "traditions of civility" in much the same way.[35] Our question here will concern the extent to which the progress ideology, whether it is espoused by a capitalist or a socialist culture, in fact sets every man's hand against that of every other and undoes the very reason for one man's hand being distinct from that of another.

GOOD INTENTIONS

There are many cruel twists in the history of good intentions in the progress culture. Progress in the health sciences and agriculture triggered a wild growth of human population. Catastrophic results were not long in following. While many continue to assert that "no one dies of overpopulation," overloading the planet with people, as Garrett Hardin noted recently, makes such disasters as that of Bengal virtually inevitable.[36]

The natural laws governing populations are many. But one underlying principle dominates them all. It is the simple fact of physical space. It says that any sustained increase in numbers of any organism of any kind brings it ultimately into collision with the limits of its living space. Since the surface of the earth is finite, so inevitably is the number of humans that can live on it. Despite proposals advanced to expand the carrying capacity of the planet by cultivating jungle land, watering deserts and farming the seas—most of these are ecologically naïve, nonsensical proposals—the spatial limits of the earth's surface are real and unavoidable. The limit of population on the planet is fixed by square mileage.

We can expect something like the Bengal disaster to result from the so-called "green revolution." While this revolution has temporarily enabled some Asian countries that formerly imported food grains to export them, it has not been accompanied by a parallel revolution in birth control. The overall effect of the "green revolution" will assuredly be more people, and more people almost certainly means greater abuse of the planet's carrying capacity. John Calhoun recently warned that as the world's population reaches a level of about five billion people, periodic die-offs of a billion people at a time may be projected, and such disasters would have far more traumatic effect upon the modern complex cultures than the Black Death had on medieval cultures.[37] The brutal simplicity of such arguments as those of Calhoun has generally been ignored or soft-pedaled by progress ideologists, especially by true believers in the traditional sciences and technology.

The present malignant growth in human numbers is especially bitter because it is the side effect of good intentions in medical and agricultural science. The actual effect of our progress in these fields has been to reverse the survival value of ancient beliefs about fecundity and lineage, love of large families, the instincts of mother love, the desire of men to sire progeny. These deep natural drives have been made mean. They have split our nature into rival factions more implacably opposed than anything Saint Paul imagined. Natural man is driven to reproduce; rational man has made it suicidal to follow this urge.

Something similar has happened with war. Science and technology have made war something that it never was before. The qualities of stamina, courage, stealth, bravado, the capacity to survive infection from battle wounds, had positive survival value for many thousands of years. Tribal conflict and the test of strength in ancient arenas and medieval tiltyards strengthened and selected men of courage, ferocity and prowess. Suddenly the value of such traits has been inverted. Courage, daring and bravado were necessary in primitive combat. They can prove catastrophic in a warrior placed before a computer console controlling ballistic missiles.

Such contradictions, however, are characteristic of a self-amplifying system of beliefs such as the progress ideology. It has produced one tangle of tragicomic events after another, specialists stumbling into each other like fat men colliding in a doorway, squabbles about the value of DDT and an odd inability to even conceive that evil can follow from conflicting good intentions. Highway technology pumps carbon monoxide into our central cities and then health scientists scurry about, measuring resulting brain damage. A smog science emerges in which as much money is spent researching the content of filth in the air as is spent trying to stop it at its obvious sources. An agrochemical industry achieves massive increases in harvest from the land only to find that fertilizer runoff destroys the harvest from the lakes and streams. Airports are located in flat swamplands where landfill technologists can work efficiently. Then wildlife specialists are called in and told to do something, for heaven's sake, about the impending extinction of wetland birds. We have only recently begun to appreciate what this means managerially. It means that unpredictable side effects of the decisions within subparts of a highly developed managed culture can easily nullify good intentions and efficiently precipitate a disaster.

One need but consider the possibilities of three sets of good intentions, each designed to make for progress, each, however, generating first-, second-, third-, fourth-, and fifth-order side effects. As the distance between each good intention and its side effect increases, predictability decreases. By the time good intentions interact in the zone of their fourth- or fifth-order side effects, their consequences are virtually impossible to predict, let alone control. If the effect is good, we announce that we have "lucked out"; if the effect is bad, we call it an accident, or disaster, depending on its magnitude.* But the difference between a fortunate side effect and an unfortunate side effect is that we can survive good fortune. Russian roulette, too, is a game involving side effects. Suicide, however, is one side effect most of us find unacceptable.

The irony of all of this is that the idea of progress is so saturated with the swagger and conceit of our species that we now seem blind to the treacherous inversion of good intentions that can result. Science and technology are still shaped by the chest-thumping attitudes of primitive man. Learned men puff their pipes as they apply game theory to war, measuring first-, second- and third-strike capacities, like some latter-day Pangloss, missing the point apparently that the earth is a sphere and that after a first strike the wind will take care of retaliation. Biochemists announce that they are about to solve the riddle of life, once and for all. Computers whir and make stupefying predictions of life in the future, the arrival of surrogate mother surgery, love machines, more of everything. It is all part of the progress ideology, natural and inevitable,

---

* One of the more interesting devices for catching unique events on the wing is the Center for Short-Lived Phenomena, founded in 1968 at Cambridge, Massachusetts. It records information on earth-science events, e.g., earthquakes; biological events, e.g., oil spills; astrophysical events, e.g., meteorites, and such events as No. 100 of 1970, a typhoon in the Bay of Bengal.

with man its elect vehicle. Everywhere we hear the boast that the "mind of man" can extricate him from any disaster it may have gotten him into, as though he had planned to get into trouble in the first place. It is all very odd, remarkable and depressing.

Social stress indicators are so numerous and well documented that I will reiterate only a few here—the apparent rising crime rates, rising costs of health care, sordid warehouses for our aged, the drug problem, the rise of the anti-hero and dandy as models for the young, empty city treasuries, increasing frequency of strikes by critical public employees such as police and waste-disposal workers, rapidly rising costs of public welfare, the strange increase in the numbers of lawsuits against computer companies whose machines disgorge great tangles of confusion as their complex systems magnify error,[38] even overload problems in the government's new surveillance techniques that threaten to transform security files into caricatures of what a self-respecting police state requires.[39] As for the growth of science, one need only note plaintive reports that some wild monkeys are now becoming scarce enough to threaten laboratory experimentation—an especially touching footnote to our newfound concern for life on the planet.[40] But the transformation of our large cities into vast sinks of cultural vitality—*Newsweek* recently called Manhattan "pruriently squalid"—is one of the most ominous crisis indicators of all.

Strictly managerial crisis indicators are also abundant, in both the public and the private sectors. We see evidence of federal political power irreversibly shifting toward the executive—even as information overload in interagency communication within the executive branch reaches an alarming level —helter-skelter governmental social programs, hundreds of patchwork solutions to urban problems, periods of administra-

33

tive panic followed by apathy and resentment when brave new ideas falter. In the private sector, we also witness fits of managerial anxiety, hell-for-leather efforts at expansion, bankruptcy of major industries, painful retrenchments and then pilgrimages to Congress for further subsidies—once-proud captains of industry resembling poor Henry IV standing barefoot in the snow at Canossa seeking the forgiveness of Pope Gregory VII.

To be sure, modern cultures have generated material wealth on a scale that ancient cultures could not have imagined, and we parade these riches at world fairs like Ashurbanipal returning from the sack of an enemy city, caravans groaning with spoils. But this material wealth is a thin, ephemeral thing. All of the wealth that exists as goods and services today could support only a sixth of the world's people at the present level of life in North America.[41] And it does not change matters to define wealth as skills stored in the human mind if these skills are attached to the progress ideology. Whether preached by New Deal liberals, conservative Western industrialists or Soviet zealots, these beliefs rest upon the same economic assumptions, the idea that the planet is like a roast pig distended with riches, and that man was licensed by fate to devour it and then, like some bellowing glutton tossing the bones of his feast over his shoulder, move to another orgy. We announce plans for a $1,485,000,000,000 economy by 1980[42] and the Russians announce their "Great Plan for the Transformation of Nature." [43] Both the Russian and the American scientists speak of reversing massive arctic river systems to water deserts thousands of miles to the south.[44] And now, as the capstone to such lunacy, we hear proposals to "seed" Mars with microorganisms so that it will develop an atmosphere and become ripe for human assault,[45] as if we could simply rid our planet of its trouble by moving it to another. The dangerous aspect of this kind of thinking is that within a totalitarian society it is virtually without controls, and within a system of free institutions it continually escalates as politicians vie for favor.

Population growth and scavenger economics imply a hardened *Realpolitik* in international relations and the increasing possibility of wars. Tensions and conflict rise along with scarcity, and the increasing reliance of major powers on resources outside their national frontiers has obvious and frightening implications. A kind of Boyle's-Charles's law of social relations is involved. As resources are depleted, the stronger nations toughen their policies and collusion becomes more sinister. Arms must be distributed studiously among weak nations so that they take their frustrations out on one another. Have-not nations must be coached in the use of propaganda, litanies of hate and false hope. But the possibilities of irrational outbursts increase at the same time. Recent calculations seem to indicate that the time devoted to war, as measured by nation-months, has been amplifying in gigantic oscillations of peaceful and violent periods since the beginning of the last century.[46]

Another feature of the hardened *Realpolitik* is that there will be need for scapegoats for the death of progress. In some nations, they will be industrialists, former heroes of the booty age. Even now in the United States there is a rising level of conflict and contention about who is responsible for the continuous rise in the cost of living when, in fact, much of this rise is related to resource depletion and the costs of environmental abuse. The scapegoat may become the scientist and the intellectual, some of whom appear to be party to unnatural acts taking place behind laboratory doors. It may be the technologists who convinced us that we could have a man walk on the moon but now, after that epic event, begin to fade from public favor amidst apologies for not having seen

35

these events within the framework of larger human earthly needs. It may be that special kind of scientist who is bent on development of artificial intelligence and, as he does, invents means by which misery, "neuroses" and conflict can be deliberately engineered into dumb machines.

It is possible that the scapegoat for the death of progress will be a familiar minority. As unemployment rises, it may become the Negro, with our troubles being blamed upon parasitism of our inner cities. Or, as the Jew's prominence in intellectual life and civil protest is brought increasingly to the public's attention, we may witness revived anti-Semitism. Possibly the scapegoat will be the aging New Left, or post-hippie movements, though these movements may be protected by their instinctive appreciation that what is happening to the planet violates life. Beneath their tantrums and regressions is a scumbled kind of nature worship, and they do not make demands upon the planet which the progress ideologists have made. Moreover, these movements seem to be turning in a medievalist authoritarian direction. They may be a harbinger of the culture we will be forced increasingly to accept.

The so-called generation gap is real, but it is basically a scapegoat-seeking phenomenon in which the progress culture displaces its anxiety on the counter-culture and the counter-culture does the reverse. The generations are shouting across a gulf caused by the collapse of the progress ideology. The resentment on both sides is instinctive. Both realize that what the other stands for is a symptom of its own predicament. The "neat" or "straight" world of business and industry knows that the counter-culture stands for an end to its beliefs in unlimited production and unlimited growth. It knows that the slovenly ways of hippie youth are both a rejection and a threat. It knows too that its continuous compromises and concessions to the younger generation are a mixture of real concern and anxious make-believe. It tries desperately to court its young, it makes them "the finest generation we have ever seen"; it lowers the age of legal adulthood and appoints them to boards of regents and boards of trustees. But it knows that much of this is a charade, a plastic solution. As for youth, they do not really understand why surfeit sickens them, only that it does, and so their songs wail "Look what you have done to me." And their slouching, unkempt habits are the result of the same anxiety suffered by their parent generation: an inner realization that they are not living true to themselves.

III

THE DECAY
OF MEANING

THE WORD "BARBARIAN" is derived from the term *barbaros,* a word used by the ancient Greeks to denote the seemingly senseless babble of tribes they considered coarse and uncivilized. But Arnold Toynbee has suggested that barbarians can appear inside as well as outside a culture. Where the external barbarian pounds at the gates of civilization with battering ram and war club, the internal barbarian insinuates values and habits that degrade civilized life from within. I interpret much of the so-called counter-culture we witness about us today as evidence of such internal barbarism. It takes the form of vandals scratching obscene graffiti on the wall of a synagogue or a courthouse; it is a mass of middle-class youth milling about at rock fests, knee deep in the rubbish of spent affluence; it is the faddish imitation of primitive dress and body paint. In the drawing room, it is the fad of affectation and compulsive vulgarity and cynic devaluation of tradition.

To be sure, coarse manners, slopping one's soup and barnyard humor have always been an element of rural and lower-

Selections from this chapter have appeared by permission of the publisher in *Human Organization,* 30 (Fall, 1971), under the title "Niche Defense Among Learned Gentlemen."

class urban culture, and there is a candor and vitality in these blunt ways. It is the vitality of van Gogh's drawings of peasants and miners of the Borinage in contrast with the sugared titillations of neoclassic paintings of nudes for the École des Beaux-Arts. But the new vulgarity in America is not that of the Borinage. It is a forgery. It is the titter of middle-aged audiences at X-rated films; college youth of affluent background attending classes dressed as men who work with their hands; the simulated poverty and stylized indolence of the hippie. It is an attempt to steal character rather than earn it. It is the sloth of a vocabulary whose highest reaches are scatological monosyllables. It is Jerry Rubin's *Do It,*[1] with its mixture of voluntarist grunts, banal "revolutionary" yawp and obsessive pornographic photography. *Do It,* with its fanaticism, its close-up photographs of infant genitals and its political prurience, has, in fact, a chilling similarity to the kind of barbarism that typified the writings and photo albums of Nazi concentration camp managers.

The significance of such documents as *Do It,* or the "new freedom" in film, or the "new honesty" in literature, does not lie in their shock value. The shock has long since dissipated. Their significance is that they betray gross and alien values, bellowing curses from beyond the walls of civility. They are evidence that something has gone out of modern Western civilization, that something is also insinuating itself through every breach in Western ideals. They bring to mind images of goatskin-clad Visigoths stumbling among the ruins of ancient Rome, draping themselves with loot, grinning as they urinate at the base of empty temples in the Forum. These symbols of Classic ideals had no meaning to such men. They could only scratch their vermin and gape at the world in ruins.

LEARNED BARBARISM

One cannot but be impressed, the more one ponders the matter, that many of the problems that now sorely try our learned professions are rooted in the "now" mentality of the barbarian *Do It* world. There is the same "in" derision of ideals, the same narcissistic preening. There is the shortened sense of time that we associate with barbarians who cannot defer gratification, the same perverse pleasure in regressive behavior. In psychology there is a "revolution in feeling" [2] and "humanist" psychologists are found at their national conventions somberly considering the therapeutic merit of predatory sexual use of patients by therapists.[3] Science takes on the quality of a cerebral game, what the young have called an ego trip, in which amorality masks reality. J. M. R. Delgado, for example, describes the therapeutic wonders of brain implantations by which a monkey, a bull or a human can be stimulated to feel extreme pleasure, or rage, by remote control. He tells us of the ingenuity of patients in designing wigs and hats to cover their wired skulls:

> Leaving wires inside of a thinking brain may appear unpleasant or dangerous, but actually the many patients who have undergone this experience have not been concerned about the fact of being wired, nor have they felt any discomfort due to the presence of conductors in their heads. Some women have shown their feminine adaptability to circumstances by wearing attractive hats or wigs to conceal their electrical headgear, and many people have been able to enjoy a normal life as outpatients, returning to the clinic periodically for examination and stimulation. In a few cases in which contacts were located in pleasurable areas, patients have had the opportunity to stimulate their own brains by pressing the button of a portable instrument, and this procedure is reported to have therapeutic benefits.[4]

Delgado says that one of the goals of his work is to make it possible to relieve patients suffering from epilepsy and the misery of acute anxiety of their terrors by wiring and stimulating their pleasure centers. Who would deny Delgado's desire to do good? But his motives are those of the "children of light" of whom Reinhold Niebuhr spoke, more sentimental than cynical. They are those of the naïve idealist. But Niebuhr also notes that the idealist is forever victimized by a tendency to "look for some immediate cause" of man's perennial inclination to do evil as willingly as good.[5] This is the very center of the barbarism of modern intellectuals. They do not, or cannot, appreciate that "children of darkness," the moral cynics who delight in intrigue, venality and the design of death camps, thrive among us because they understand the foolishness of the children of light and the ease with which self-interest among men can be put to use toward cynical ends. Thus we find in Delgado's work only passing discussion of how whole classes of men might be wired so that their docility and rage centers could be put to use by moral cynics. The full meaning of his work lies half hidden.

One of the underlying causes of the new barbarism with its frantic search for meaning in the present, as I suggested earlier, is the deep, pervasive need to escape the destructive demands of hyperrationality in an era when the progress ideology is losing its hold on the modern mind. The progress ideology was, after all, a secular substitute for earlier Judeo-Christian views of why men live. Like those earlier views, it placed man in a vertical and superordinate relationship to the rest of nature. But there were profound distinctions between the effects of the two outlooks on life. As the belief in a hereafter lost its grip upon us and the wonders of science and technology came to occupy a central place in our attention, the future as a spiritual certainty, an eternity into which both good and bad

41

were all to pass, became blurred and ambiguous. The progress ideology temporarily lifted from modern man any real need to think about the future, except in short-range materialist terms. It seemed also to remove any need to fear the future. In America, an entire generation grew up with but the dimmest notion of what death could mean. Since progress was natural and inevitable, death was a kind of temporary inconvenience for which science would provide a solution. Even now, biologists suggest that once they have unraveled some mysteries concerning the behavior of free radicals in the chemistry of the cell they will be able to arrest the aging process. So the future became an ever-receding mirage, a sort of glimmering oasis on the horizon in which happy, cola-quaffing people gamboled, half breathless in anticipation of the next technological marvel. After the flying machine and electric light there were plastics, and after plastics artificial hearts. What would they think of next?

The result of such experience is radically reduced historical depth perception. Like a jeweler's eyepiece, it intensifies concern for things immediate at the price of long-range vision. It links the arrogance of progress with myopia, and produces a "now" culture that markets hot pants and litters Yellowstone Park with equal avidity. It produces feminine-hygiene deodorant sprays and battery-driven sexual stimulators, "theater" as a calculated "now" regression—the James Joyce Memorial Liquid Theater—fast-buck housing and disposable everything. It produces those "decent godless people" of whom T. S. Eliot spoke, "their only monument the asphalt road and a thousand lost golf balls." The old values, such as "patch it up, wear it out, make it do," values that made good ecological sense, are turned into the "arts of consumption," as Stuart Chase calls waste.[6] This view of life made garish ecological atrocities certain, and it is now possible to predict that by 1980 strip-mining will scar an area almost the size of Connecticut, Maryland, New Jersey and New York combined.[7]

Management of "now" barbarism was inevitably obsessed with tactics, and indeed that is what is so characteristic of the managerial revolution we associate with Frederick Taylor, Henry Fayol, Elton Mayo and their recent counterparts. It deifies efficiency and makes the "practical man," the short-range thinker, its champion. To be efficient is to be virtuous, and to be efficient in the short run is assumed to be a virtual guarantee of progress in the long run. For a hundred years, in fact, the managerial literature unrolled as a single great paean to the virtues of "efficiency." If the organization is beset with communication overload, Program-Planning-Budgeting techniques are recommended to get out of the difficulty, even though, as Victor Thompson notes, it may only mean more frantic accumulation of useless information.[8] If the planet is scourged by oil spills, the response is sensitivity training for oil company employees. Or, as things continue to worsen, we computerize something else, which makes for more confusion between the real world and hyperrational abstractions. Meanwhile, powerful natural correctives come into play to remind us that we cannot live despoiled lives and that self-delusion survives only in the theater.

Something else happens to make the world of science and technology into a "now" phenomenon. Specialization slices experience into "data" and quantification flattens experience to where one "fact" is as important as any other "fact." The world becomes a nominalistic caricature, a spatter of events, each unconnected with the other, each contextless, like beads fallen from their string. Quantification destroys the ideological cohesion of experience, and knowledge turns into a perversely empty thing; and it soon becomes impossible to determine which scientist is doing something significant and which something trivial. It levels distinctions between ordinary and exceptional men. This is why science and technology have become such singular expressions of modern mass-man culture, able to absorb thousands—even tens of thousands—of men of limited talent, as well as crude ethical sensibility, at the same time that they exhibit the arrogance peculiar to the specialist, the arrogance of the "learned ignoramus," as Ortega y Gasset called him.[9]

The symptoms of this decay of meaning are particularly obvious in information factories, especially the universities. Because they have been seen by the lay public as a place where the progress ideology was especially self-evident, they have experienced spectacular growth. Student enrollment jumped from something over a million in 1930 to just over two and a half million in 1950 and to five and a half million in 1966. This was seen, surely, as another illustration of progress. Expenditures, too, have increased stupendously, from something just over a half billion in 1930 to about fifteen billion during the same period.[10] Federal money flowing into the universities increased at a similarly spectacular rate, from about a billion in 1960 to five billion in 1970. Daniel Moynihan recently suggested that the dependency of the universities on federal money was now so great that few could survive serious reductions in it.[11] He also noted that, despite prodding by more than one President, leaders in the universities seem unable to think configurationally about their institutions, unable in fact to even appreciate the magnitude of the problem they confront. I suggest the reason is that they have been overwhelmed by specialization.

Trouble in the universities has received a great deal of attention but usually for the wrong reasons. At times, certainly, they have seemed on the verge of complete collapse, or paralysis—which is collapse in an upright posture, therefore less immediately apparent. If buildings are going up, it is assumed that the value of what goes on within them is also rising. Thus costs have skyrocketed, research budgets have become bloated, sometimes by grants from donors with dubious motives. Great hives of capricious faculty specialists have sprung up, but the man of traditional liberal-education values has become harder to find. The once-serious task of teaching has declined in prestige and fallen into disrepair. Support of the arts and humanities has declined in comparison with that of science and technology, and the accumulation of information becomes a substitute for cultivation of wisdom. Students who seek liberal education find it almost impossible to piece together a meaningful sequence of studies from the fragmentary world of specialist faculty. Unless the student is prepared simply to lose himself in the atomized world of the learned ignoramus, he turns in outrage upon the system demanding that it be torn down and reassembled—for instance, that wholesale reform of the grading process be initiated—or he walks away in disgust.

The inability of universities to respond flexibly toward their problems because of their fixations on hyperrational pursuits is especially obvious in undergraduate teaching. It is generally conceded that such teaching is seriously neglected, and that student contact with senior faculty is brief or trivial. But curiously enough, confronted with this situation, and in the face of established facts of motivational psychology, undergraduate teaching is still used as a form of faculty punishment. Junior faculty and graduate students must endure large amounts of it while prestigious senior faculty do little.

The solution to such problems is suggested by the medieval university where tenure did not exist as we know it, where students hired and fired their faculty and where teachers were sometimes required to post bond from which fines for poor

45

performance were deducted. In the present situation, the answer would seem to be a piece-rate wage for teaching undergraduates. Quality controls might be a simple system in which good students evaluate teaching after completion of courses. The effect of such a scheme would probably be immediate. Senior faculty would demand the right to participate in the ennobling educational process; good teachers would be attracted into teaching, and poor ones driven out. It would loosen the grip of the publish-or-perish rule on faculty survival, reduce redundancy in libraries and tend to flush superfluous personnel from costly research posts. To protect teachers working in exotic pockets of the knowledge industry, such as the teaching of extinct languages, a minimum wage could be set. This implies, to be sure, that scholarly pursuits are not all of equal value. But in a world where the unknown is infinite and the resources for studying it are finite, this should be no surprise.

Many irregular incentive systems are already in use in the universities. There is moonlight teaching, night overload wages and the semi-illicit use by one university of teachers from another. But this contraband traffic in teaching is an indication of the value distortions of these institutions, evidence that they are indeed in trouble.

The curiously muddled and wooden condition of the universities was never more evident than during recent episodes of campus violence. They responded with tragicomic bewilderment, at times with armored vehicles and bayonets, at other times with ritualistic self-abasement of administrators and at other times with frantic debasement of entrance requirements. The entire display was reminiscent of General Rosecrans's response to defeat at Chickamauga. "He acted like a duck hit on the head," as Lincoln put it.

To understand the helplessness of a modern university, one must examine its characteristics as a natural community. A close look at a large university's organization, its dominant values and fugitive functions, reveals that it is very much like a natural community of less loftily motivated organisms. Its flat, collegial structure, for instance, has very early origins. So does its structure as a self-governing community. In 1229, when students at the University of Paris rioted to protest costs of living, as well as the quality of wine in local taverns, Pope Gregory IX issued a bull granting students and clerics full authority to regulate their own affairs, including the right to suspend classes. Relative communal autonomy of the universities continues to the present day. A modern school of the Big Ten variety will have several hundred governing bodies, senates, codification committees and the like within it, along with countless *ad hoc,* departmental and sub committees— seemingly monumental bureaucratic confusion. But when we look at universities as natural systems we find that they are vast niche volumes occupied by throngs of specialists, and that the relations of these specialists to one another are meticulously regulated by a complex web of symbiotic, commensal and host-parasite rules.

The capacity of the modern universities to resist change and absorb punishment is related to this ecological diversity. Each committee and subcommittee, and each senior faculty member, has veto power—to some degree—and it, or he, can oppose change more easily than facilitate it. Each such veto response is a small negative feedback loop which helps damp out major variation in behavior within the total community. These small regulator loops are similar to those regulating other complex ecological nets.[12] This is why the renowned liberalism of university faculties is seldom related to university

47

self-interest but is usually directed outward, toward off-campus affairs, toward such problems as world statecraft, on which an intrepid posture is as safe as it is impressive.

University organization seems to be codified confusion on an absurd scale. Actually what we overlook in such an interpretation is that while the overt functions may be confused by a tangle of amendments to amendments, many covert functions actually thrive in such situations. These covert functions are the private interests of faculty and administrators. The interests of each faculty member, department, committee and subcommittee are regulated within a web of community controls, a complex of miniature control loops, the strength of each being its veto power, the capacity to say "no!" to any proposal threatening change.*

The precise manner in which the ecology of a university produces conservatism is illustrated by faculty search-and-screen committees seeking candidates for administrative posts. Two things tend to dominate their thinking: scholarly productivity and leadership vitality. Few men of high scholarly achievement have had opportunity to study or practice modern administration. Their experience is generally limited to the clerical chores of departmental work. But scholarly achievement normally indicates that the candidate has lived within faculty culture long enough to absorb its dominant values; for instance, the conviction that trying to apply any cost-benefit formula to faculty performance is absurd.

Evidence of leadership vitality is not usually seen as an

---

* There are interesting social-psychological dynamics involved in the negative, often peevish, posture of faculties. The notorious sense of powerlessness of intellectuals who feel that their gifts are fully appreciated only by God generates a powerful need to demonstrate identity before their fellows. Existentially there is obviously a greater sense of Being if one acts as a valve rather than a mere pipe in the flow of decisions. To say "no!" means to say "I exist!" But this response heightens the problem of the intellectual who has difficulty distinguishing valor from petulance.

asset in a candidate but more usually as evidence of an authoritarian or illiberal inclination. Hence, candidates who survive screening are often tractable administrative amateurs who are willing to accept faculty culture as it is, and whose scholarly achievements are limited enough to assure docility in the campus environment. It is difficult for catholic, visionary and vigorous men to come to the surface under such circumstances. If they do, their administrative half-life immediately becomes a prominent topic for faculty club analysis. They soon run into trouble, or resign, whereupon placidity once again reigns in the faculty community.

The modern specialist in a university is the product of a modern dilemma. Because life is short, he can only achieve eminence in a field by sacrificing breadth for depth, and normally he cannot take time to entertain synoptic ideas. Moreover, specialist societies reward him for preoccupying himself with a very narrow band of experience.[13] This is what produces "received opinion." Since it has powerful influence on mimicry habits, it is a force to be reckoned with. One is reminded of Lord Rutherford's observation that talk of atomic fission as a source of power was "moonshine." The fact that he was wrong is not important—anyone can be wrong. What is notable is that two of his colleagues promptly concluded the same thing; one "confirmed" his calculations, and another thanked him publicly for calling a halt to "wild, unbridled speculation."[14] This sort of thing, to be sure, is common in any specialty. But it underscores the fact that expertise carries a price. Expertise amplifies natural human vanity by giving the specialist a deceptive sense of power and authority when he takes part in prodigious collective feats; e.g., lunar exploration. Leslie White, the anthropologist, once alluded to this problem by making the droll observation that the Nobel Prize was sometimes given for discoveries that required imagination of about the same order needed to open a "recalcitrant jar of pickles." [15]

I do not wish to cast aspersions on talented men in the sciences. I merely wish to stress that a community of specialists, such as is found in a university, produces its own kind of pigheadedness, the kind that greeted Rachel Carson with condescending derision when she published *Silent Spring*. Such professional set is common in most of the sciences. In anthropology there is the story of the intense skepticism and ridicule which Raymond Dart and Louis Leakey met when they first noted evidence that Australopithecines used tools.[16] The fact that the expert is often ignorant of the side effects of his recommendations within the progress culture is what now makes him so dangerous ecologically.

The modern specialist is perhaps no more heir to natural vanity than other flesh. But his expertise amplifies its dangers, and when it is joined with that of others in the mutually reinforcing predilections of professional societies, it can be an extremely potent force. It is this quality that enables the barbarian specialist, as a pesticide chemist, for example, to recommend dumping huge amounts of DDT on farmlands without appreciating the destructive side effects. Needless to say, perhaps, this is true of both physical and social scientists, especially as their expertise is invited during formulation of public policy during the present crisis in our culture.

The progress ideology within the universities, and for that matter in the information industry generally, has produced oddly contrary habits. An enormous volume of information is generated, but as this volume grows,* symptoms of overload appear. Unpublished research findings are backed up in dis-

---

* No one really knows the number of scientific journals and periodicals published world wide. But it jumped from about 100 in 1800 to 5,000 in 1900 to something like 27,000 in 1958, and perhaps 75,000 today. As this

orderly queues; data are abstracted to where caricatures replace reality ("model-building," for example, becomes more and more fashionable) or new information is simply ignored —in other words, treated as meaningless. These overload symptoms have been studied in many other systems—by James Miller, for example—and they are very similar to what is so obvious in the universities.[17] It is as if the volume of information in the universities were losing its glue, as if we were confronted with a great ball of lint composed of bits of information on everything, from glottal stops to enzymes, little of which seems to help us meet the moral problems of everyday life, of ghetto poverty, oil slicks, butchering seal pups or decent treatment of the aged.

Evidence of very similar overload problems in communication technology generally is indicated by the rising frequency of lawsuits against computer companies whose machines mistakenly erase vast amounts of vital information, or spew out confusion as error reverberates through interlocking sub-systems. There is also an increasing frequency of ludicrous blunders in critical communication systems affecting national security, such as the recent case of a false alarm of an enemy attack being broadcast through some parts of our private broadcast system because one gentleman in a key position in the sequence "reached up and took the wrong tape off the hook." Then, too, there is the comic-opera manner in which information has often been indiscriminately collected by military surveillance agencies and pumped into national data banks concerning subversion.

---

bulk of information increases, so apparently does the probability of its recombination in new inventions and discoveries, so that the growth of this corpus of information has been almost logarithmic. Computerization contributes, of course, to this acceleration. That the acceleration cannot continue indefinitely seems evident.

Student riots, demands for "relevance" and the growing public doubt about what it is getting for its money from the universities are more evidence that the hold of the idea of progress is weakening. We must bear in mind that whenever the question of "relevance" arises it is really the question of priorities for the use of limited resources that is at issue. Some of the public anxiety now directed at universities clearly has its roots in anxiety about science and technology generally. Despite vast expenditures in the sciences, to many laymen our problems seem to be increasing, not diminishing. Poliomyelitis has been "cured," but now the public media inform us that control of such "disease" has intensified the population crisis. Transplant surgery has saved lives, or at least lengthened some, but it has also ushered in lurid new ethical and legal problems. Science-based technology took us to the moon, but it also gave us multiple re-entry nuclear bombs. Part of the public disillusionment with the sciences appeared because science has been seen by the average man for many years as the cutting edge of human rationality. It was believed to be uncommonly well honed in men of learning in the universities. Yet it is within the learned community that the decay of meaning seems to have begun first and is often most glaring, as professors join mindless mobs, rake the culture with every kind of epithet and remind the ordinary man that as far as support of the universities is concerned he has been betrayed.

While the ordinary citizen does not appreciate what is going wrong within the universities and has no real understanding of why the disarticulation of meaning in our body of knowledge threatens to defeat further efforts to enlarge it, he does know that costs are getting out of hand and that faculties are often self-centered and presumptuous. He also sees that as money gets tight there is increasing disagreement within the university about how it should be spent. Questions of relevance come up, and faculties begin to point the finger at one another. The hard scientist accuses the home economist of being lightweight, and the social welfare educator questions the cost of a still larger linear accelerator.

The reason for the noise is that niche defense is usually a raucous affair. The situation on the campuses is not unlike that observed by ecologists in the study of mealworm communities. Granular stratification of meal allows competing forms to coexist reasonably well side by side. Mixing strata destroys the rules and results in lethal competition.[18] Lessening financial support in a university upsets its rules of coexistence in the same way. So do efforts to reduce duplication in curricula. The so-called establishment in a university is its set of ecological regulators. The action of these regulators is often expressed in various beliefs about what universities are for.

Many definitions of the uses of universities have been put forward over the years. Most are familiar. They are said to be places where the heritage of our culture is passed along to the young, or where the young go to learn how to make a living in the professional world. To others, universities are places where faculties have time to think, where the truth is pursued without fear or favor, assuming the pursuer is tenured. In the minds of some, it is a place where faculties have time to ruminate on the ethical problems of life; for example, on the shortcomings of public officials as moral animals, the assumption being—at some risk to modesty—that academics have mastered their own. To some, universities are places where the quest for knowledge is rather like a religious calling, and just as the monk helps pray the ordinary man into heaven and expects support for it, the scientist or scholar makes progress possible for society and lays a claim on the public purse for doing so.

Then there is also the view that universities are places

where truth is pursued "for its own sake." This is a more complicated idea than first appears, and its effect on universities is often not fully appreciated. The idea now rests on the notion that curiosity is a good thing, and that if a little curiosity is good, more of it is better. Curiosity and progress are seen as mutually dependent and necessary.

It would be fairly easy to demonstrate that curiosity has survival value because it keeps the individual alert. Innate releasing phenomena have been demonstrated among the higher orders of animals in which very little, if any, external stimulus is required to initiate search behavior. Curiosity in man may be rather like this. But at the same time it would be difficult to demonstrate that the need to know is as intense among all people as we find it in the West. Most cultures have traditions, dogmas and various party lines that control the need to know. Such beliefs operate as cultural inertial-guidance devices. They act as negative feedback controls and minimize pitching and yawing in institutional life. The Yir Yoront, to whom I referred in a previous chapter, used its mythical past in this way. But the idea that truth is pursued "for its own sake" has particularly odd effects. Its casual reiteration is an indication of its mythic quality. From an epistemological point of view, the problem is clear enough provided one accepts the ideas of Peirce; namely, that any opinion, idea, belief, theory or habit has consequences that determine its survival value. The meaning of something utterly unknown cannot be determined in advance; nor can something utterly unknown be pursued. Pursuit of knowledge "for its own sake" amounts to senseless pursuit of the useless.

Actually, most specialists pursuing knowledge "for its own sake" are inadvertently relying on Veblen's definition of a university as a place where "idle curiosity" is subsidized.[19] Being a technocrat and progress ideologist, he was, of course, attracted to such a view, but in our times this is a very vulnerable argument. Efforts to demonstrate systematically that "pure research"—which is one traditional description of the exercise of idle curiosity—has useful consequences have proved unconvincing, apparently even embarrassing. *Science* recently published a note describing how one such attempt to do so failed and had to be "quietly buried." [20]

But our modern need to quench the thirst for knowledge is a hypertrophied form of curiosity, a lust that feeds upon itself and produces its own after-the-fact justification. When this lust dominates other values in the culture, it can be a dangerous thing indeed. We in the West not only display a need to know more about the surface of Mars, we also need to know more about the use of hypervirulent microorganisms in germ warfare, and we also, of course, need to know how long we can keep hopelessly decrepit patients alive in our hospitals by connecting them to assorted pumps, tubes, filters and bottles. Certainly if science-based warfare or science-based search for ever greater GNP is any guide, we have to consider the possibility that the need to know, as we understand it now, may be a lethal cultural sport, our vaunted objectivity the kind of pointless composure an executioner might display as he adjusts the hangman's knot beneath his own ear.

Karl Deutsch comments on the systemic effects of curiosity in an especially insightful way:

> Curiosity may lead to drifting; the new discoveries or data are accepted as highly important regardless of their probable consequences for the integrity and autonomy of the individuals or organizations who acquire them. Rapid increases in knowledge . . . may overload the steering arrangements and steering capacities of the [system]. The result is the partial or total loss of self-determination.[21]

What all this means is that cognitive disarticulation of

knowledge within the knowledge industries is an analogue of the retreat from consciousness in the *Do It* world. The existential absurdity of a completely "factual" world actually drives the specialist toward more unquestioning obedience to hyperrational fixations and *Do It* barbarism. It produces the world of Camus's *Stranger,* in which "everything comes to the same thing," including murder. It produces a world where hyperrational equations substitute for moral definitions, a world in which it is possible to torture animals to quantify pain and to torment men in order to measure the torment.[22]

Please observe the regressive *Do It* quality of what occurs in such cases. Scientists, all presumably decent men, make self-imposed species-wide amnesia the first premise of "now" utopia:

> The immanence of control technology depending, as it does, on our attributes as machines, makes it irrelevant any longer to debate the ethical or political implications of where we came from. . . .[23]

This is why scientists seem to collide almost by accident with the concept of evil, as though it were a mean and bewildering prank in their world of clean abstractions. "After all," says one researcher working with artificial intelligence, "the human brain is just a computer that happens to be made out of meat." [24] Hyperrational barbarism is the world of Artificial Intelligence research where "men who contemplate infinitesimal riddles of circuitry . . . never look up from their work to wonder what effect it might have on the world they scarcely live in." [25] But it is a world where a curious, Eichmann-like morality reigns, where a scientist can say as he quietly continues his research,

> I have warned . . . again and again that we are getting into very dangerous country. They [the federal agency financing his work] don't seem to understand.[26]

56

It is also the world of research on test-tube babies in which the question "What are we going to do with the mistakes?" meets the defiant response, "We will do our transplants and go on with our work as we decide, not as anyone else decides." [27]

UNKNOWN GODS AND PERTURBATIONS

Camus once observed that the ultimate question for man was suicide. In a very basic sense, the remark indicates the grand illusion of our age. It is a half-truth, a species-centric comment, rooted in the same smug assumption that fueled our vulgar rampage across the face of the planet. It rests on the assumption that man, this strutting, puffing, assertive biped, is the measure of all things, the final marvel of creation, his extinction therefore the ultimate philosophic issue. Plainly there is more to the matter of ultimate questions. The ultimate question is whether man, with science and technology harnessed to his vanity, will drag all of life to perdition with him. The question is whether man will carry all of life to hell by some ghastly miscalculation. Such a fate would foreclose the possibility that another species might evolve better suited to be the vehicle of life's pilgrimage toward full awareness. The possibility of such a foreclosure is the ultimate question.

Saint Paul reports in Acts 17:23 that the Greeks to whom he preached in Athens had erected, among the main altars to their gods, an altar to the Unknown God. They did so on the assumption that not all of the gods had been identified and that it was wise to take no chances with the unknown. It was a singularly keen move, one that stands alongside Pascal's wager as eminently sensible. For only the rashest man will assume that he need not fear the unknown. Yet it is the failure of modern hyperrational man to assume that there are permanent and unavoidable limits to his knowledge that now threatens him with a disastrous fate. Disguised as a claim to ultimate rational omniscience, a kind of modern secular Pelagian outlook crept into the modern mind. The unknown came to be viewed not as something to which one pays homage, something to be approached in awe, but something that is almost perversely elusive, something that must be driven from its lair by relentless research. But Unknown Gods rule over the unpredictable in science and technology, too, over those events that are sometimes quaintly referred to in scientific usage as "perturbations." And perturbations usually arrive unannounced, as the grim companion of good intentions. So it is with dam-building. The Aswan Dam has not only failed to fill with water as rapidly as its engineers predicted, because of the porous limestone surrounding its basin and high evaporation rates; sedimentation processes in the Nile Valley have changed; bilharzia infection in tributary canals has increased; delta salinity has increased and the seafood resources in the area have been severely damaged.

The way in which side effects lay waste good intentions is often stark and pitiless. There are numerous illustrations in the history of primitive cultures such as the case of the Yir Yoront, the primitive Australian society I mentioned earlier. The metal axe was introduced to this culture by missionaries in 1915. Previously they had no knowledge of metals, and they fashioned axes from stone with handles hafted to the stone with bark cord and gum. Since their home territory did not possess the stone they needed, an extensive system of coastal intertribal trade among pairs of male traders had evolved in connection with the manufacture of axes.

Within the tribe, the axe was borrowed from its adult male owner by women and young men in a highly regulated way, and a complex set of social relations, including totemic rules, initiation rites, as well as regulations of male, female and family roles, came to surround use of the axe. As missionaries began to distribute steel axe heads in the nineteen-thirties among the females and youth receptive to mission beliefs, a series of side effects shook Yir Yoront culture. Trade relations with neighboring tribes were disrupted; the authority of elders was undermined; male-female roles became confused; ceremonial and formal leisure activities disintegrated. The Yir Yoront became a ragtag clutch of poverty-stricken people whose very physical survival was threatened.

One can identify more complex side effects of good intentions at work by examining cases where one set of side effects collides with another, nullifying the positive value of both. During recent years, there have been numerous programs sponsored by Western nations to assist East African countries to develop economically. One scheme includes the ranching of strains of imported Western beef. But these animals are susceptible to sleeping sickness spread by the tsetse fly. The ranching schemes have therefore seemed to require indiscriminate slaughter of wild game that might act as vectors for the sleeping-sickness organism. But extermination of game outside park areas has intensified native hunting and poaching forays into the parks, and game herds in the parks have declined. As the park herds decline, so does their value to tourism, a major industry in these nations. Yet the same donors that have assisted the ranching scheme assist in building roads and first-class tourist hotels in the parks. The net effect of the two interacting sets of good intentions has been to hurry the extinction of wildlife, to upset the regional ecology and to lower the quality of native life.

The Yir Yoront and the East African cases illustrate how destructive the use of good intentions can be. The metal axe head seemed to the Australian missionaries an obviously desirable means for improvement of everyday living. They did not see the axe as something whose very meaning was defined by its context of use. A "fact" in that case, too, was construed as an obvious thing, like the use of beef to meet protein deficiencies in East Africa. The possibility that a whole series of side effects, an unknown context, would be associated with it was not really grasped. This is what has so often happened when scientific information has been taken as ethically neutral, something that can have meaning apart from any context of use whatever. This is why good intentions have such a notorious ability to surprise us by turning upside down, producing the very opposite of what they are supposed to produce.

The evil that may lie hidden in the penumbra of good intentions is illustrated also in current American experience. A former research chief in the Pentagon was recently quoted as saying:

> When I was director of Defense Research and Engineering under President Eisenhower I believed that some chemical and biological weapons, especially the non-lethal variety, could be usefully incorporated into our defense arsenals and might, in some degree, make war more humane. I have come to realize that the situation is very much more complicated than I had then thought it was. Indeed, these weapons generally make war more inhumane especially when used in conjunction with conventional weapons. I consider my earlier support of biological and chemical weapons to have been perhaps my biggest mistake of that period.[28]

In the same spirit, a team of Harvard scientists announced a few years ago the successful isolation of a single genetic function from a segment of DNA of the intestinal organism *Escherichia coli*. The striking thing in this case is that, unlike Robert Oppenheimer, who came to "know sin" after the horrors of Hiroshima and Nagasaki, the leader of the Harvard team "knew sin" from the outset. He was quoted in the press as saying:

> I feel that the bad far outweighs the good in this particular work. I feel that it is more frightening than hopeful. It is obvious that it raises the possibility of genetic engineering.

A colleague added, "We don't necessarily have the right to pat ourselves on the back." [29]

It is worth noting that while the Harvard team realized that the "bad far outweighed the good" in their work, they nonetheless felt constrained to open Pandora's box, to push the advent of genetic engineering closer, as if goaded by unseen forces, perhaps the fear of being accused by colleagues of committing a Luddite heresy. The compelling thing in such situations is that ethical issues are obscured by a progress principle and the fiction of the amoral act. The scientific fact— the scientific act—is removed from its ethical context and given a special moral immunity, like the military man who justifies commission of an atrocity on the ground that he follows orders. Obviously there is more to the question of genetic research than "science." It is not only a question of what genetic diseases might be brought under control; it is also a question of what kind of creature we now choose to become. Is the design of our species to be decided by referendum, simply by the curiosity of geneticists, or by a laboratory-born lust to commit the sin of Faust? Does the creation of new intelligent species for use in "low-grade labor," as some scientists now predict will soon be possible, require another abolitionist struggle? Having set aside in the sciences, as mere rhetorical exercise, the question of when during the long processes of evolution man received a soul, are we now prepared to decide the point at which we will deny our laboratory-engineered congener the right to claim a soul? The comments of the

Harvard geneticists seem a feeble plea indeed before the gods that rule the Unknown.

In a world where we seek to plan and manage our way out of desperate straits by imposing some small portion of will upon events, we have paid a high price for refusing to look upon the nature of man realistically. Again, take the matter of war. One of the great hazards of our time is that we will continue to treat war as a perturbation, something accidental. We ignore the fact that man has evolved in a butcher yard, that he has been at the business of war, butchery, depravity and deceit for centuries on end, with a dedication unknown to other species. If we are to study man with historic honesty, he cannot be seen as some helpless victim of predatory warrior minorities, or munitions makers, or class struggles, some poor creature whose heart is in the right place, a mere victim of circumstance. He must be seen wading in the blood of his own kind, shrieking obscenities, boasting of his captaincy over the universe and occasionally on his knees racked with remorse. It is not enough to point out, as some social scientists like to, that there are cultures—e.g., the Eskimo—that do not know war. For the Eskimo, peace is a demographic restraint, not a matter of virtue. It is difficult to get enough Eskimos together in one place to have a war, and there is plenty of evidence—in their suicide rate, for instance—that Eskimos are no exception to the powerful self-destructive forces that lie deep in man's being.[30]

I say these things not because they are some unhappy announcement that fits a private bias but simply as a reminder that modern man's nature is not a benign, but unfortunately pervertible, thing. It is the product of a long struggle to hack and bludgeon his way to dominance in the animal kingdom. The fact that he lacks the instinctive controls on his aggression which normally accompany the development of dangerous natural organic weapons (fangs, claws, horns and the like), and that therefore the invention of artificial weapons poses the direst kind of threat to him, is one of the strange things that paleobiology demonstrates all too clearly. These are obviously considerations which must be taken into account in any realistic assessment of "human nature." After all, that man can excuse himself from the laws of biological heritage that apply to all other life simply to please his romantic sentiment is a notably dangerous presumption. This is not to say that because war comes easily to man it is inevitable, only that because it comes easily to him he must be aware of his vulnerability and build the protection he needs against self-inflicted collective violence.

IV

THE
RETREAT FROM
CONSCIOUSNESS

CERTAINLY IT IS EVIDENT that something is wrong in our modern culture. We experience its contradictions and paradoxes every day. The rationality of modern science and technology has flung open the doors of the universe and we have been shown a world we never dreamed of in the past. But it is not the universe we had hoped for. Science was to have given us something more reassuring, not this thing woven of gauzy provisionals. Technology was to have been more yielding in its service to man. Yet the incessant questions of science and obdurate presumptions of technology have not only flung open the doors of the universe; they have thrust us into a trembling hall of mirrors, an endlessly receding chamber of doubts in which questions outrace proof and reassurance. The deeper we press our questions, the more certitude recedes from us, so that the information we gain about the universe does not lessen the fright of existence; it intensifies it. The future has become an apprehensive thing, a tablet blurred by gloomy runes, and our deepest instincts warn us of what they will tell us if we decipher them. It is not surprising that most men recoil from the possibilities of so unsure an enterprise.

ABSTRACT EXISTENCE

The uncertainty of our condition is the result of our having replaced the assurance of tradition and its underlying organic confidence with abstract estimates. It is a feeling that has been growing for several hundred years, a remorseless development that is compelling to contemplate. This was first impressed upon me by Ortega y Gasset's essay, "Point of View in the Arts," in which he observes:

> The guiding law of variation in painting [in the West] is one of disturbing simplicity. First things are painted, then sensations, finally ideas.[1]

And truly, Ortega's law seems to run like an iron rod through five centuries of art, from the pre-Renaissance, the Renaissance, the chiaroscurists, impressionists, cubists, expressionists, on down to the op, pop and the conceptual art of the last few years. It represents the relentless rationalization of aesthetic experience and a shift in the West's world view. Perhaps this shift seems clearest in the arts because art is the most prescient side of human culture. In the arts, man shows what he is long before he knows what he is.

Many writers have commented on the trend toward abstraction in the arts. In 1906, Wilhelm Worringer observed that the tendency toward abstraction seems to be motivated by anxieties of an uncertain life, and that among some primitives abstract forms and patterns are used to "establish a stable world beyond the world of appearances" to reduce the "torment of perception." [2] In a harsh and uncertain environment, he suggests, men produce abstract forms, and in a more benign environment they turn to natural forms and an empathy with nature, and produce "objectified self-enjoyment."

Worringer's thesis may seem oversimplified, just as Ortega's law may seem too facile. Yet its basic point is provocative. Certainly in the West there is evidence of the steady movement during recent times toward abstraction in the arts. There is "gradual depreciation" of edge and tangibility in painting,[3] and the appearance of such schools as cubism in which the artist attempts to combine a variety of experiences in a single perception, freezing the flow of experience in a single abstract conception.[4] The influence of rationalism was more direct and obvious in other ways, such as in the effect of spectrographic research on impressionism and Orphism, and in the camera's impact on representational art in general. The result of these many developments was to place a "ban on pathos," [5] and to replace the object with rational constructs.

The quest for rational absolutes has dominated the evolution of painting, architecture, interior design and landscaping in the West for at least two hundred years. It culminated in the work of Piet Mondrian and Ludwig Mies van der Rohe. Mondrian's career as a painter was preoccupied with a desire to purge the "tragic" from art, to eliminate the organic by the use of the "primordial" right angle and straight lines—for him the straight line was the "fulfillment of the curve." [6] This same search for absolutes led Mies to attempt to design buildings that were "triumphs over reality," buildings that could be assembled from basic modular forms not dependent on the exigencies of site, function and climate.[7] As with Walter Gropius, buildings were to be "normed." [8] Thus the slab form, "a form proper to our age," emerged in architecture as the expression of its dominant modern spirit—for the hyper-rational age what the medieval arch was for its time.[9]

The straight line is a symbol of predictability, the signature of hyperrational existence. It is a puritan curve, an idea basic to the purge of emotion. It is the *sine qua non* of such temples to hyperrationality as Chicago's O'Hare Airport. The O'Hare buildings are places where machines are tended as altars were tended in other times, places where faith is expressed in a reliable flight schedule and where individuals queue up for absorption by secular rules of life. Although such fiercely rational buildings are sometimes seen simply as the final solution to kitsch, they are not. For they engender a powerful counteraction, as we easily detect if we examine the nostalgic décor of the barrooms and restaurants in these buildings. These dimly lit bars and cafés are retreats from the hyperrational. Their wood veneers and synthetic antiques indicate just how stingy normed buildings become and how desperate is our need to smuggle feeling into them.

It is the hyperrational spirit that imposes the tyranny of the straight line on the silhouette of our cities and makes the "modern" city park or plaza an abstraction more to be seen than felt. This is why modern urban design is best appreciated from the air. It is also why we cast benches for our parks as abstract sculpture and thereby indicate that they should be looked at, not sat upon—the ultimate indignity, no doubt, to the foundation of our organic being. It is why we design furniture as though the arm were a fleshless hinge and the lumbar curve a boorish refusal to accept the canons of good taste, why we erect transparent buildings that alternately expose the inhabitants to sunburn and to voyeurs. We submit to these indignities as churchgoers once submitted to the chastisement of hardwood kneelers. The significance of the straight line in art and architecture is not that it is "clean," but that it is consistent with the values of our time, those of quantification, computer print-outs, the processing of men by turnstile. It is a mistake to assert that we erect glass box architecture—or "package space," as it is sometimes put—because it is cheaper to do so than to put up buildings less monotonous in form or sterile in detail. It is particularly wrong to argue that a nation as wealthy as the United States can only afford stingy buildings. Were wealth not seen in abstract terms—as the play of the marketplace, Dow-Jones averages, "investments" and the like—we would not insist upon buildings that express the same spirit. We would not suppress the need for organic beauty beneath the rules of abstract existence. Form continues to follow function and in a way it always does, but the function of form in a hyperrational age is use of man as an abstraction.

Abstract existence is implicit to modern experience across the entire range of modern scientific and technical activity. In physics, Albert Einstein and Leopold Infeld have described the shift in viewpoint from mechanistic principles to those of field and relativity theory as the object of research dissolves into ever more abstract rational constructs.[10] Jung notes that psychology took form as a science in the late nineteenth century as a corollary of the dissolution of institutionalized guides to life.[11] In sociology, abstract existence expresses itself in endless statistical measurements. One could almost rephrase Ortega's observation to say, "First things were studied by science, then sensations, finally ideas." The external world has been dematerialized, and meaning is drawn toward and into the self.*

A similar shift can be traced in the development of organization science. At the turn of the century, Frederick Taylor's "scientific management" concerned formal organizational

* Interestingly enough, Toynbee notes that as we trace the evolution of main characters in Shakespeare's plays, they "etherealize," with Henry V a creature of events about him, Macbeth a creature of external events and his own nature combined and Hamlet a study of the internal conflict within the hero's soul. (Arnold Toynbee, *A Study of History*, abr. D. C. Somervell [New York: Oxford University Press, 1947], p. 201.) I leave it to the reader to consider the many implications this sort of change within an artist has for a theory of collective recapitulation of individual psychological development.

problems, division of labor, command principles and the like. Luther Gulick and Lydall Urwick, among others, pushed these ideas further toward questions of planning, staffing, organizing and controlling.[12] By the nineteen-thirties, an era of efficiency experts arrived, but even then attention began to shift toward subjective considerations. Men such as Elton Mayo and F. J. Roethlisberger became concerned with social and psychological factors of industrial life, problems of morale, motivation and group interaction. The neo-scientific management that has emerged since Taylor's work is, of course, more sophisticated than anything Taylor knew, and it takes hyper-rational form as operations research, queueing, information, game and decision theory. However, it does not nullify or oppose the human relations school. It absorbs it into a more resolutely abstract view of institutional life.

POP RELIGIONS

Our modern time of troubles is visited, to reiterate a point I made earlier, by strange new paradoxes in the life of our culture. While the principles of science and technology reign supreme and a web of predictability has been spun around great areas of life that have always seemed mysterious and beyond comprehension, there has been a simultaneous destruction of tradition's hold upon us. It has opened a void in the rules of existence. Paul Tillich speaks of an "emptiness and meaninglessness" in our age;[13] Karl Jaspers observes a radical disillusionment with "overconfident reason";[14] Martin Buber notes wild oscillations of public mood, an "intoxication with freedom" followed by a "craze for bondage." [15] The steady rationalization of experience has generated a powerful resistance to it.

Resistance to rationalization takes form as resistance to

universalization, as reaffirmation of the particular. It runs counter to the notion of normed life, quantification, mass duplication; that is, predictability. Its spirit is embodied in Hans Arp's maxim, "I forced myself to contradict myself in order to avoid falling victim to my own style." Such responses are a refusal to be normed—always, too, in part romantically nonsensical. One is reminded of Geoffrey Scott's account of the Englishman Beckford's instructions to his architect. He asked him to design "an ornamental building which should have the appearance of a convent, be partly in ruins and yet contain some weather-proof apartments." [16] This foolishness may seem outlandish when we look back on it, but it is more. It shamelessly inserts those humanizing foibles into experience that hyperrationality neither understands nor tolerates. When such men as Gabriel Thouin published books depicting various fake ruins a patron might erect in his garden, and when landscape architects planted dead trees in the Parc Monceau near Paris, they were not only pandering to a fad among gentlemen seeking a "simple life in satin slippers," [17] a life that required evocation of sweet melancholy, they were also reasserting the feeling of time in human experience. The frigid formal styles of the preceding period reflected the rationalistic fixations of their age, and these fixations tended to minimize this sense of time and mortality. The romantic landscape architects assuredly went to extremes, but they did grasp the need we have for organic identity, and the dead trees they planted and the garden ruins they built indicate just how far men will go to hold on to their sense of organic reality. That sense is ultimately rooted in realization that we are mortal, and when hyperrationalism attempts to smother or gloss this realization men will go to almost any length to resecure it.

In architecture, this same resistance to the hyperrational is expressed in Antonio Gaudi's wild and writhing forms; "In

God's architecture," he said, "there are no straight lines." [18]
In Le Corbusier the same impulse is found and he relied on
"passion" as an antidote to collective principles.[19] In Frank
Lloyd Wright, it is expressed in a love of the thought of Lao-
tzu as well as his use of rock and unfinished wood.[20] But
Wright's case illustrates how the romantic spirit can at times
infiltrate the hyperrational ethos, only to be changed by it. For
while Wright's inventions—the tie-rod connected concrete
block, cantilevered form and such—were quickly absorbed
by modern architecture, many of his organic principles were
soon vulgarized for mass production, as with the "picture win-
dow" and cloying excesses of lannon stone in the suburban
ranch house. While Wright was strongly influenced by organic
Asiatic art, these Asiatic ideas did not survive in America in
the romantic form in which they influenced him. They survived only where they were consistent with the hyperrational
spirit. Thus the abstract principles of Zen art appear in Isamu
Noguchi's "gardens" in the plaza of Chase Manhattan Bank
and at Yale's Rare Book Library. These gardens are fully abstract expressions, cordoned off, meant to be contemplated
from a distance, like the renowned dry garden of Ryoan-ji.
One does not enter them physically, as one does in walking
the steppingstones of Heian-Jingu. For the dry garden attempts to purge the "tragic" in much the same way that Mondrian did, by deriving meaning from the "pure plastic," from
space, the *sunyata,* abstraction. Their artists turned to use of
sand, stone and evergreens in the same spirit as Mondrian
when he rejected the "tragic" trees of Paris, preferring the
concrete and straight-line forms of Manhattan.

Mies van der Rohe's buildings are cold for the same reason.
His forms, like those of a dry garden, were intended to imply
permanence, and they were made cold to put them beyond
the reach of uncertainty and insinuations of mortality. While

it is true that many later architects have tried to add warmth to their buildings, it is a cosmetic thing, an afterthought that masks affect-hungry abstraction. But this conflict of the mask and the reality hides the deep conflict between modern urban life and our organic nature. For urban life is necessarily normed life. Modern cities are places where efficiency, predictability, bus schedules, abstract rules govern everything we do. They are places where records must be kept, computers tended, streets paved, where snow is a costly enemy and rain a nuisance to be quickly shunted into sewers. It is a place where trees are imprisoned in concrete pots, where plastic flowers thrive and men "keep" hours.

Man's instinctive resentment of the modern city as an anti-natural thing manifests itself in a hundred ways. When people reared in cities are asked to recall their most pleasurable childhood experiences, they do not conjure up images of pristine high-rise buildings or miles of sidewalk pavement. They recall images of the trees they climbed, the hideouts in the bushes they fashioned, earth they tunneled. They "rarely conceive of the city as something that might give pleasure in itself . . . as if a mild civic nausea were a normal burden of man's [urban] existence." [21] I think, indeed, that much of the destructive force of urban mob politics today is rooted in this revulsion and much of the romanticism that infuses the politics of urban violence is linked to organic deprivations that accompany rearing young in apartments, on asphalt playgrounds, in parks where the grass is fenced off, in a world cut off from the roots of man's organic nature. Man evolved, after all, in a world utterly different from what modern urban life has made it.

Abstract existence is a peculiarly contradictory force in our lives. It calls, as Mondrian said, for a "cultivated exteriority," along with a "deepened and heightened interiority." [22] The

72

deceit of such a double life is now clear all around us. As our established institutions have decayed, we have retreated to an ever more subjective definition of reality. Yet simultaneously science has been brought to bear upon everything we do, and it drives us from our subjective refuge. Even the most intimate human experiences become subject to public examination. We find white-smocked research scientists soberly collecting "data" by motion picture on changes in color of the genitals during intercourse.[23] But "cultivated exteriority" drives human subjective needs, the needs for privacy, personal integrity, to ever more desperate and furtive recourse. Ultimately, man rebels, and the rebellion often takes form as a "counter-culture." [24] The essential of such counter-culture is its retreat from consciousness. It is not a new, heightened consciousness, as Charles Reich argues in *The Greening of America*. His "Consciousness III" and its "childlike, breathless sense of wonder" is a psychologically regressive condition.[25] It can take vicious forms. There is certainly more than childlike wonder among the hippies we see on television news broadcasts beating "Jesus freaks" on the streets of London.

The retreat from consciousness follows the collapse of a great central belief of our era, the belief in endless progress. That is why the retreat involves all ages and classes. But we cannot retreat to traditional values and beliefs, to temples that reek of dissension and decay. We must invent new gods and raise new temples. The retreat seems most dramatic among the young, because its antihistorical quality is most obvious in the age grades that suffer most acutely from the cultural amnesia brought on by a violent scientific and technical break with the past. This is why the young are so bombastic and tedious in their assertion that the present era is new, unique and utterly different from what has gone before. It is also why they persist in announcing that they have invented the political

73

wheel, that things will be different now that they are with us.

But the wild tangle of perfervid beliefs, gothic deformities and comic pomposities of youth are simply part of a general process of cultural search and invention. Thus there is the hippie movement, with its gypsy dishabille, bare feet, buckskin, simulated poverty, fountain play and political fantasy. There are pop religions, astrology, yoga fads, black magic, witchcraft and cults of murder.

The current interest in the work of the Marquis de Sade and the sex-sadism fixations of the counter-culture are not, of course, just coincidental with the preoccupation of "in" vocabulary with excrement and the rhetoric of national self-abasement. It all hangs together, at times frighteningly well. Witness the reported remark of a young female Weatherman at a Flint, Michigan, meeting in which she comments on the ritual murder of civilians in California by the Manson "family": "Dig it. First they killed those pigs, then they ate dinner in the same room with them, then they shoved a fork into a victim's stomach. Wild!"

Then, too, there is constant talk within the counter-culture of our "lost sense of community," the need for "communitarians," "participatory democracy" and "all power to the people." [26] There are messiahs of radical politics whose heaviest cross is a TV talk show, revolutionary "philosophies" whose only substance is a suppurating foul mouth—coprolalia, as the psychology of insanity terms it. There are "underground" newspapers whose protection by the First Amendment is romanticized as a special kind of curse. It is as if revolution were confused with a cure for acne.

Then, of course, there are cries for sexual "liberation." That counter-culture responses are often associated with the sexual "liberation" cause is notable. For the hedonism of much of this "liberation" is a self-centered overcompensation betraying deep personal anxiety in an age of uncertainty. The pathology of the homosexual "liberation" movement is especially obvious insofar as homosexuals protest too much. They are, after all, a sterile species—if they practice what they preach—and, like luckless mules, survive from generation to generation on the borrowed virility of others. Something similar is involved in the more militant side of the female "liberation" movement. It is clearly more than a matter of equal pay for equal labor. There is a bitter quality about it, and to the extent that it succeeds in reducing men to flaccid misogynists and makes women towers of solitary spite, it destroys itself.

Although the hippie movement has a great deal in common with bohemian responses of earlier decades—e.g. post-World War I Dada—it began to take distinctive shape in this country after World War II with the "beat generation." It was a kind of pop existentialism that included pietist and contemplative elements from Eastern thought. But its basic orientation was retreatist, with use of alcohol and marijuana, mood folk music and cool jazz.* Its dress was drab, often entirely black, and its hair style was straight and bedraggled. It was restricted to small colonies in a few cities and its political mood was lethargic.

What is significant about the beat culture is the manner in which it molted and spread during the sixties as a great melee of antirational fads, tantrums, dandyism and romantic excess. Withdrawal gave way to noisy, mawkish sentimentalism, exhibitionism and fierce attacks upon the "establishment." Even

---

* The inclination of humans to use alcohol and drugs as methods of psychological escape is, of course, proverbial. But in 1922 Eugene Marais suggested, after extended observation of baboons in the wild state, that other primates, too, seem to seek to retreat from "the pain of consciousness" by eating euphoria-inducing poisons—a point that should give species-centric humanists pause. (See Eugene Marais, *The Soul of the Ape* [New York, Atheneum, 1969], pp. 117–33.)

the dominant hair style changed from "natural" stringy treatment—girls often ironed the curls out—to another "natural" form that was teased into wild, uncombed nests. Music became amplified, big-beat, cacophonous and orgiastic. A whole battery of new drugs appeared, along with a psychedelic art influenced by drug-induced hallucinations.* Dress became wildly colorful but patched and spattered with cynicism, disfigured flags, bits of American military insignia, and its antimilitarism and pacifism began to be expressed in a curious involution, the wearing of secondhand military garb, as if to imply that to hate war one should simulate the distress of combat. It is no less significant that European youth have made a fad of wearing elements of American military garb on everyday dress and that fashionable boutiques charge high prices for such items. Some analysts have seen it as evidence of antimilitarism, but others have seen in it a need of the young "to act out their fantasies as conquerors." [27] It is probable that the two motives are mixed and that each is increased by fear of the other. There is a new kind of functional hypocrisy in all of this, as there is generally in the present fashionable concern for "honesty." The studiedly filthy look and simulated poverty of middle-class hippies is not only an affront to the very society whose material surfeit sustains it; it also helps simplify experience in a world overloaded with the sensory bombardment of "now" living.

Though in many ways the hippie movement is related to the so-called "youth cult" of today, I think the youth cult has much broader significance. For while it is in large part a product of skilled commercialism—e.g., the "Pepsi generation" —its more fundamental meaning relates to the decay of established beliefs about life after death. Even though Nietzsche

---

* The absence of the straight line from this art, the absence of the signature of rationalism, should not be overlooked.

announced the death of God in 1882, the idea did not become public knowledge until the last twenty years. Indeed, hyper-rationalism managed to suppress the meaning of this deicide for an entire generation, and it appeared for some time that positivism had succeeded in putting death out of mind. But here, too, reality would not be mocked. The result is the "now" generation, a gigantic, frantic charade involving all ages. "Now" is contrived of make-up kits, instant suntans, toupees, false eyelashes, hot pants, narcotics, jogging fads and transplant surgery.

The "now" spirit bears close study. One of its central characteristics is that in it age and death are heresies.* The dead are frozen or turned into donors. The senile are put in "homes" where their decay is out of sight. Undertakers become straight men in sordid mortuary make-believe. Even the antiwar movement takes on the "now" spirit as it fantasizes a day when men no longer love to fight, when it is finally proved once and for all that "war is not in our genes," that mass butchery is the perverse doing of MacBird and munitions makers. Life must be transformed into an immortal happening and Miguel De Unamuno's assertion that our tragic sense of life comes from knowledge of mortality must be put aside with computerized predictions of the day when men need no longer die at all.[28] The "now" retreat from consciousness thus makes it possible to avoid the cup that deicide has made so bitter.

The manner in which the "now" spirit manifests itself in a culture that announces itself as atheistic is also worth noting.

* Here is what we find in an article called "The Immortalist," by Alan Harrington, in *Playboy,* 16 (May, 1969): 116: "Death is an imposition on the human race, and no longer acceptable. Man has all but lost his ability to accommodate himself to personal extinction; he must now proceed physically to overcome it." The author slides lightly across questions concerning the existential horror surrounding accidental death in such a world, a world in which "the mathematical certainty of a terminal accident" dooms everyone and "immortality" merely extends the time spent on death row.

In the Soviet Union, the embalmed body of Lenin in Red Square is a curious symbol of the dilemma of an ideology that allows for no belief in life after death. A hero is made permanent and propped up for the faithful to fix upon, like a bouquet of plastic roses, something that transcends time and death. But when a "Great Man" such as Stalin falls from grace he is furtively buried and allowed to rot. Time is allowed to claim him.

The rise and spread of the so-called sensitivity group movement is part of the larger counter-culture retreat from consciousness. It, too, has tangled roots: John Dewey's educational theories, elements of neo-Freudianism, Carl Rogers's nondirective therapy and Kurt Lewin's social psychology of the democratic group.[29] In one way or another, each represented a self-indulgent, highly subjective view of life, a life in which guilt rather than the act becomes evil, in which permissive attitudes are equated with mental health. Each exhibits what Buber called an "intoxication with freedom," and each generates a fearful vacuum of social meaning.

Sensitivity training's original intent was to increase educational effectiveness by using the potent interpersonal forces latent in classroom social dynamics. But it soon took a wide range of clinical, research and lay-group forms, and it now involves mental patients, businessmen, industrial workers, educators, civil servants and laymen from every walk of life. A hundred and one variations of the original "T group" have appeared: confrontation groups, intervention groups, marathon groups, groups that meet in the nude, kiss and tell sacraments of every kind—a "rich, wild new tapestry of intensive group experience," says Rogers.[30] *

* Here is the way the Anadysis Institute of Los Angeles describes one of its contributions to this "rich, wild tapestry": "July 26–30, July 30–August I ADVENTURES IN LOVING MASSAGE. These workshops teach the mas-

The rapid spread and proliferation of the sensitivity group movement would seem to be, however, more than evidence of the masses' desire to undertake the dubious pleasure of what Rogers calls a "painful journey to the center of self." [31] It appears, in fact, that the opposite is true, that the movement is another evidence of the current "craze for bondage" following our "intoxication with freedom" of the recent past. The appeal of the movement to the average man lies in the fact that the breakdown of traditions, especially ethical and religious, has produced a massive vacuum in social role definitions, the void of which Tillich, Jaspers and Jung wrote. The freedom to do anything, say anything, deny or assert anything, is proving an empty gift. It is as if everything in life goes up and nothing comes down, as if the romantic's belief in man's eternal innocence were a bubble, an iridescent counterfeit.

The latent authoritarianism of the sensitivity movement is underestimated by its apologists. But one should not underestimate the significance of what Rogers calls the sensitivity group's "savage" demands upon the individual to "remove his mask and be himself." [32] Such demands are demands that the individual surrender himself to the group, that he deny his historical nature, that he disown what he has learned to be and accept new masks given him by the collective. For the masks of which Rogers speaks are molded of social role. Their successful use by the healthy personality necessarily involves an ego defense system, including masks. The "psychonoxious" price the individual sometimes pays for would-be shortcuts to self-knowledge by such devices as sensitivity training can be

---

sage of caring, touching and loving as well as meditative and sensory awareness. Participants are encouraged to make this a weekend of getting *in touch with themselves*, a joy, a relaxation. Couples, friends and individuals are welcome. Nudity is a necessary and meaningful part of this workshop. (Week-long) Fee: $125.00. Deposit: $50.00. (Week-end) Fee: $50.00. Deposit: $20.00." [Emphasis mine.]

high.[33] Hence there is mounting evidence that stripping away the individual's masks may only mean substitution of a more subtle set of deceptions, new masks that rely on consensus in a make-believe world where terms like "relating" become substitutes for genuine insight and sustained friendship. Weak or neurotic individuals, or those caught in the confusion following the collapse of institutional supports such as traditional marriage may provide, are vulnerable to the powerful, often pernicious, social pressures latent in the self-abasement rites of sensitivity groups. Moreover, the sensitivity group may reinforce narcissistic self-deception by providing the individual opportunity to preen his "honesty" publicly, and it may also provide leaders opportunity to satisfy their neurotic needs for dominance. The sensitivity group can be an embossed invitation to the authoritarian to run others' lives. This possibility, indeed, is one of the reasons why there is now so much concern, though it has a hollow ring, for accrediting procedures of "sensitivity trainers."

While the degree of normlessness appropriate to various kinds of sensitivity groups continues to be hotly debated,[34] the vocabulary of the movement is laced with the language of romanticism. There is concern for "liberation of the consciousness," the need to "free the individual," the need to "grow" and the language of the "feeling realm." The assumption is that the individual is chained by the establishment, the family, the school, the organization, the "system."

The degree to which the new commune movement and the popular mainstream of the sensitivity movement share basic romantic views of human nature is very clear. The "search for self" in the one and the "search for community" in the other assume the same thing, that the individual is somehow lost. Otherwise, why the search? Both, however, are indications of the degree to which there has been a breakdown of traditional rules of social life. Both involve a mystic quest for regeneration and both presume that a valid life style is possible only after one rejects—in part, at least—the social rules of an establishment. Both assume, too, that the decay of old habits must take place before a new set of rules can take their place. Some of these rules will rise spontaneously from the group and others will be imposed. This is why there is such a striking similarity in the lyrics written for the sensitivity group movement—e.g., by Rogers—and panegyrics on the commune such as the following:

> We are entering the time of the tribal dance as we go to live in tepees, celebrate our joys together, and learn to survive. We go to a virgin forest with no need for the previously expensive media of electric technology. The energy we perceive within ourselves is beyond electric; it is atomic, it is cosmic, it is bliss.[35]

There were, to be sure, many kinds of American communes during the nineteenth century and there are many kinds today. At present, we have everything from slovenly "crash pads" that call themselves communes, in a sentimental effort to glamorize sloth, bathos and roaches, to "Drop City," where deliberate internal regulation is slight—"We used to have some rules but they never worked out." There are others such as the Lama Foundation where social regulation is recognized as a precondition for survival, where the "deep need for rules just to keep you from doing what you want" is acknowledged.[36]

Those communes that have survived, both in the past and in the present, have had to accommodate their dreams to reality. The successful nineteenth-century communes were bound together by powerful religious and ideological beliefs and headed by charismatic figures, men who were "viewed with awe by members."[37] The most obvious thing about communes past or present is that anarchism is a poor organizing principle for social life. Hence, it is perhaps inevitable that the anarchistic pronouncements of many of today's communitarian youth are also associated with idealization of totalitarian figures such as Che Guevara and Mao Tse-tung. The craze for bondage is, after all, a withdrawal symptom following intoxication with freedom. This is why there is a streak of cynicism in so much commune thinking. Just as Hulme defined romanticism as spilt religion, cynicism is curdled romanticism. The hopes for New Harmony are not new, nor is the final chapter of events there.

> He [Robert Owen] then purchased New Harmony from Mr. Rapp, and commenced his establishment in the month of May last. As he laid the foundation of it entirely on perfect equality and community of property, many enthusiasts in these principles from various parts of the Union joined themselves to him; and also a number of vagabonds and lazy worthless persons, from all parts of the world, that would willingly live at the public expense, who had drunk away the little money, if they brought any at all, at the tavern, and *who would not work, but desired to say a great deal.* Mr. Owen had gone to England on account of business in the month of July, and during his absence, a complete anarchy had been introduced into the new community. . . . He lamented over his people, and brought the situation of anarchy in which they had fallen before their eyes so plainly, with the consequences resulting therefrom, that they invested him with dictatorial authority for one year.[38] [Emphasis mine.]

NATURE WORSHIP

Though for centuries the progress ideology has been the driving force behind the changing conditions of life on earth, only in the last few decades has its impact upon the planet raised doubts about its ultimate consequences. During the last century, its presumptions seemed secure. It was a giddy time, full of invention, flamboyant militarism and optimism. Primitive and traditional cultures gave way easily before the onslaught. The African continent was reduced to a series of noisome trading posts. Most of Asia was cut up like so much butcher's beef to be parceled out by the Western powers.

But during the last century professions of faith in progress often betrayed an uneasy, self-contradictory quality. The suspicion that something was wrong with its basic assumptions kept creeping into commentary of the period. There is the following passage, for example, from the journals of Laurence Oliphant, a British traveler and Superintendent of Indian Affairs in Canada in 1854. In them, he describes his journey to St. Anthony Falls, now in the Minneapolis and St. Paul area.

> At the foot of the Falls the voyageurs launched the canoe and prepared lunch, while we explored the neighbourhood and sketched the Falls. They are only twenty feet in height; but the scenery does not derive its interest from their grandeur, but from the perfect groups of rock and wood and water on a magnificent scale. . . . We could scarcely bear to tear ourselves away from so lovely a spot. . . .

In an adjoining passage, he observes:

> But built upon the bank of the river, saw mills, foundries, shingle-machines, lath-factories, etc., keep up an incessant hubbub—delightful music to the white man, who recognizes in the splashing of water, and the roar of steam, and the ring of a thousand hammers, the potent agency which is to *regenerate a magnificent country, and to enrich himself*—but the harshest sounds that ever fell upon the ear of the Indian, for they remind him of the great change through which he has already passed, and proclaim his inevitable destiny in loud unfaltering tones.[39] [Emphasis mine.]

Oliphant did not understand that he was describing an

ideology whose appetite amplified as it fed upon itself, that the notion of "regenerating a magnificent country" was a bizarre contradiction unless the phrase "to enrich himself" was added. There was to be no slackening in this effort of the American to enrich himself at the expense of his world, until disillusionment set in.

The present disillusionment with the progress ideology began with the grisly inventions of World War I: poison gas, the modern machine gun, and life amongst the rats in the trenches. Even then, many continued to view the First World War as a perturbation, something accidentally set in motion by fickle events at Sarajevo. With Nazi death camps, saturation bombing of European cities and the atomic obliteration of Japanese cities, however, the idea of progress more obviously began to lose its hold on the hyperrational mind. The surprise is understandable enough. Had not positivists proved that the wormwood of human venality was a figment of theological imagination? After every war had not the romantic social philosophers seen a sprig of lilac growing proudly among the wheels of every rusty cannon? Above Flanders fields was not the lark still bravely singing?

But a change in public attitudes toward the idea of progress is now becoming very obvious. In January, 1970, for example, *Science* issued a special compendium of a hundred and forty papers reporting study of materials returned by Apollo 11. The issue was a monument to the triumph of scientific and technical achievement. Yet it was followed in February by a special issue of *Fortune* that seemed oblivious of the triumph. It defined the crisis of the earthly environment as our "national mission of the seventies." [40] That such a journal as *Fortune* should manifest so notable a degree of noncommercial foresight is itself significant, but some of the papers in the issue—e.g., that of Sanford Rose on recycling—make it very clear that disillusion is abroad in the progress culture. Yet it is significant that the two publications should appear at virtually the same time. It leaves one with the impression that within a few months another heroic vision of progress had evaporated. While we were adventuring amidst the sterile beauty of the moon, our home planet had turned filthy and threatening.

There are numerous accounts in anthropology to indicate that most traditional and primitive cultures have beliefs that restrain the rate of cultural change and by doing so protect the relationship of a culture to its environment. I have already noted several, the Australian Aborigines, for instance, who defined a mythic past and used it as a reference for determining what changes in living culture were to be tolerated.[41] The effect was to minimize change and maximize stability. Animistic beliefs have a similar control influence. When spirits are believed to inhabit rivers, mountains, plants and animals, the response toward the environment will be different from that of a modern housing developer.

We know from the numerous accounts collected over the years by anthropologists that most traditional and primitive cultures of the world have contained animistic beliefs which restrained the culture's abuse of the world around it. Spirits were believed to inhabit rivers, mountains, plants and animals. Before a tree was cut by the Trobriand Islanders for a canoe, or when the Ainu had killed a bear, prayers to the spirit of the plant or animal were offered that its spirit might forgive the necessity of the act. In agricultural societies, prayers and rituals of every kind were devoted to the unseen forces that insured a good harvest. The Aztec appeased the god of spring, Xipe, by dressing a priest in the freshly flayed skin of a young victim sacrificed for the occasion. Even in high cultures such as preindustrial Japan, an intricate set of rituals was woven into the everyday relationship of man and his natural environment, and to this day we find in the art of the Japanese garden unequaled reverence for natural beauty. By paying homage to the mystery of the life force, such rites, rituals and beliefs have a negative feedback influence on man's relation to the world. They breed respect, a sense of awe and reverence toward nature, and it acts as a brake on our use of the environment. The contrast between our attitudes toward nature and those of primitive man are put eloquently by an American Indian quoted by Roszak:

> "The white people never cared for the land or deer or bear. When we Indians kill meat, we eat it all up. When we dig roots, we make little holes. . . . We shake down acorns and pinenuts. We don't chop down trees. We only use dead wood. But the white people plow up the ground, pull up the trees, kill everything. The tree says, 'Don't, I am sore. Don't hurt me.' But they chop it down and cut it up. The spirit of the land hates them. . . . The Indians never hurt anything, but the white people destroy all. How can the spirit of the earth like the white man? . . . Everywhere the white man has touched it, it is sore." [42]

In the West, ever since the notion of progress took firm root, our ideas have taken a different turn. Man is made in the image of God, and when God is secularized, man is made in Progress's image. Nature is to be carved and enjoyed as he sees fit. The only animal attributed a soul is man; other creatures are "dumb." Horses exist to pull the plow, the fox exists to provide sport for the hunter; the donkey was given us by God that it might be flogged to and from the village market. The whimper of animals trussed for slaughter is a meaningless sound, from a thing that neither feels nor thinks nor dreams nor, once dead, comes to sit on the right hand of God.

The present popularity of the ecological movement among

the young is a reaction against these beliefs. There is a new religiosity in these movements. Thus the most widespread symbol of campus ecological associations is a circle overlaid with an "e." Pamphlets explain that the "O" (circle) in the symbol stands for organism, oasis, om, omnipresence, Orphic, ontology, the mandala and the four elements of the ancient alchemists. The "e" within the symbol symbolizes earth, Eden, evolution, enlightenment, eros, emotion, ecstasy, the equinox and the "transcendent unity that pervades all dualities." But the same religious overtone is reflected, in fact, in more mundane calls to ecological action by public officials. The seventies is to be a decade "preoccupied with life and the quality of life." Thus the following resolution of a congressman:

> I pledge that I shall work to identify and overcome all that degrades our earth, our skies, our water and the living things therein. . . .[43]

The significance of youthful college ceremonies in which new automobiles are buried as repulsive pollutants should not be missed because students arrive at such events in convertibles. Nor should the cynical backlash against the romantic assault on the establishment deflect attention from their significance as cultural change indicators. These events foreshadow massive economic and social dislocation, a deep, pervasive ethical change and a jarring confrontation with the laws of energy use.

The significance of the flight from the city by "New Pioneers," though obviously romantic, is part and parcel of what I am describing; thus the *Wall Street Journal*'s story of a "homesteading" family that "carves a farm by hand from Maine forest, hauls water, shuns technology":

> When Sue and Eliot Coleman sit down to eat in their tiny one-room house, they use tree stumps instead of chairs. When

87

they need drinking water, Sue walks a quarter of a mile through the woods to a fresh-water brook and hauls back two big containers hanging from a yoke over her shoulders. And when the Colemans want to read at night, they light kerosene lanterns.[44]

But, serious as the Colemans' effort to recapture the good life appears to be, one must wonder what would happen if large numbers of urban dwellers attempted to do the same. The test would then become whether or not such families were prepared to accept the radically heightened infant mortality and the radically reduced adult longevity of "homesteading" in an overpopulated country.

The rising interest in ecology is doubtlessly the most important single element in the retreat from consciousness, because it points toward a merger of science and nature worship. It implies values that are the opposite of those of the progress culture. "Subversive science" is subversive because it rests on a set of values that have a negative feedback influence on technological meddling in complex natural processes.[45] It opposes indiscriminate "development" of land and rivers. It opposes the megalomania of technical specialists. It is conservative in spirit and rests upon an almost primitive view of man's place in nature. It assumes that man is shaped by forces far larger than he is and that unless he is held in check by a fear of the gods he will run amuck. The new ecological view is thus laced with a redeeming element of nature worship. It is a Hudson River school of science. It is suffused with the appeal of J. R. R. Tolkien's vision of the Shire, a place where men live lovely haunted adventures free from the tyranny of the hyperrational.

V

BAD MEN AND
TIMES OF TROUBLE

EVEN THOUGH Jean Jacques Rousseau relied more on sentiment than sense when he cried, "Man is born free; and everywhere he is in chains," it is true that the substance of society
is social role, and institutions unceasingly try to shape men to
fit the roles society requires. Society increases collective predictability by extending the reach of roles. It feeds upon the
energy of individuals as it does, and to assemble its institutions
it draws upon the ontological substance of individuality. Individuals are its throughput, like the particles of light that ener-
gize life at its most fundamental levels. For institutions, too,
are ruled by the laws of entropy, and to stay the drift toward
decay they relentlessly suck up the free acts of individuality.
It is this energy that drives the engine of social systems.

But when the collective order weakens or collapses, when
a culture enters a period such as Arnold Toynbee calls a "time
of troubles," roles lose their hold on acts and a flurry of free
particles of unpredictability is unleashed. These acts lie toward
the edges of social control—often, indeed, outside the reach of
institutions altogether. The unique quality of such acts lies in
their historical character, the fact that they cannot be duplicated. The meaning of free acts lies in this historical quality.
They are, as Karl Jaspers says, "an origin in time . . . the

individual as historicity." [1] They are chance made incarnate by acts of will. Inevitably their essence is moral decision. So it is not strange that our present time of troubles should be marked by a great, half-blind lunge toward morality both among hyperrationalists and in the counter-culture, as well as among minorities struggling for social justice. These events are not accidentally associated. They represent a massive, spontaneous effort to re-establish the primacy of volition in a world where the principles of cause and effect have leached existence of moral significance.

THE LUNGE TOWARD MORALITY

In the hyperrational world, the lunge toward morality first appeared in the hard sciences. As I have suggested, physicists came to "know sin" shortly after the horrors of Hiroshima and Nagasaki. Biologists began to discover the concept of sin in the laboratories of biological warfare research. Geneticists are now blundering into it as they stand in the vestibule of genetic engineering. Because the hard sciences had always held themselves aloof from moral issues and taken pride in the ease with which they could pass along ethical problems to politicians, military men and clergy, the shock was bound to be considerable. For while they groveled with such unquestioning, almost atavistic, zeal before their stainless-steel gods, they unwittingly sharpened the problem of survival to so elegant, so deadly a point that only a Manichean would have appreciated the irony of their condition from the outset.

There is something almost poignant about the bewilderment of scientists unable to elude the moral world we are all caught in. When words like "evil" and "sin" became unfashionable because of their theological loading, the scientist and the moral being were caught within the same skin. The torment became especially obvious when the scientist professed liberal values, for while he was able to exorcise the demons from science it remained all too obvious that problems of social injustice, brutality and predation remained. Laboratory researchers were able to use the mythically neutral fact to disguise an amoral principle of taking orders. Until recently, the evil lurking within any notion of such work was obscured with pedantry and quantification. Yet maltreatment of minorities, abuse of weak nations and the slaughter of animal species to extinction cannot be so easily hidden. One result is a contorted double standard among many of the learned; e.g., invasions of weak nations by Western states are denounced as evil, invasions of weak nations by powers outside the West remain matters of cause and effect. Moral imperatives have nonetheless crept back into learned discourse through the crevices of such sophistry. The attempt to make every man his own moralist has produced entire professions of tormented amoralists.

Now the social sciences are discovering sin, and they, too, turn this way and that in an effort to deal with it. Alvin Gouldner recently completed a lengthy and thoughtful study entitled *The Coming Crisis of Western Sociology*.[2] In it, he attempts to deal with the decay of hyperrationalism in sociology and the impending rise of what he calls "reflexive sociology," a social science that does not see the "layman" as something to be studied but rather someone to be joined. Gouldner's work will probably be read by social scientists and few others. Even now, a mud slide of pedantry threatens to bury it.* But it is

* One reviewer of Gouldner's study had this to say: ". . . the work also provides a general and encompassing method for the contextual understanding of any 'paradigmatic' change (the critique of social theory) and suggests a sensitive and perceptive approach to the intellectual consequences and critical assessment of sociological crises in praxis and in theory (a reflexive and radical stance)." (Bob Scholte, a review of Alvin W. Gouldner's *The Coming Crisis of Western Sociology*, Basic Books, N.Y., in *American Anthropologist*, 73, no. 2 [1971]: 308.)

symptomatic of a "new sociology" that refuses to set moral issues aside for the comfort of well-constructed matrices or sets of correlations.

Fierce debates are also now preoccupying the ethics committee of the American Anthropological Association. The "subjects" of anthropological research have become no less vocal. An Indian Ecumenical Conference was held, for example, on a Crow reservation in 1971 at which native and Christian religious leaders passed the following resolutions: That perversion of sacred Indian dances for commercial purposes be discontinued; that secular use of peyote be discontinued; that the Park Service, universities, highway departments and Corps of Engineers stop the desecration of Indian religious monuments and that many sacred relics now in museums be returned to Indian tribes.[3]

The Crow reservation conference illustrates once again the dilemma of the scientific community, in this case anthropologists. The response of the Indian is like that of a Catholic priest refusing pushy positivists permission to bug the confessional for research purposes. The Indian is no longer willing to accept the scientific ideology as a set of values superior to his own. He now says that some things are more sacred than science. At the same time he asserts the rebirth of Indian will. It is not surprising that such responses produce consternation within the scientific community and that debates about the ethics of science should now appear so prominently in the literature.

The lunge toward morality is very clear in the "power" rhetoric of minorities. With constant use, shouts such as "Black power!" "Red power!" and "All power to the people!" become rather trite. But they mean nothing more or less than a reassertion of will power. They are exhortations to everyman that his identity is found in voluntary acts, that a cause-and-effect theory of life reduces men to things and living decays into an intolerable malaise. For in a world ruled by causality there is no place for will, and where there is no place for will there is no place for good and evil, and where good and evil are not realities it is meaningless to speak of human dignity or indignity. This is the root principle of some of the new "intentional communities," groups that deliberately organize themselves with articulate ethical rules. Intentionality is defined by John Bennett as the "self-conscious planning of group life with careful consideration given to the corrupting effects of relationships with the Outside." [4] The term "corrupting" is the key term in this definition. It puts the moral issue flatly before us. Who shall determine what is corrupt?

The most ominous thing about the *Do It* barbarism in the learned community and the retreat from consciousness more generally is that they are fusing into a massive collective phenomenon. This collective regression is forming a vast pool of mindless energy that waits to be directed by a few men prepared to resist attrition of their consciousness. They may then consciously channel its flood, seize the energy of the mass and chain it to a totalitarianism more unsparing and more sure than anything we have seen before. The making of such men is what I shall now examine.

SELF AS HISTORICITY

The human organism comes into the world a raw bundle of biological disposition. Most of what it is is shaped by heredity. But even the fetus is a social thing, in part. Immediately upon inception, a social-chemical discourse with its mother is under way. The mother's social experience can affect the child even while it remains in the womb. But at birth, child-rearing practices immediately begin more obviously to shape, knead and pummel the organism into the form society requires if it is to live among its fellows successfully. If the process is reasonably successful, as it usually is, the product will be an Arab, a Jivaro, a Tchambuli, a Comanche or a Republican Methodist American, as circumstances require.

The personality is a complex thing. We can visualize it in only the crudest sense. One may do so by imagining a ring within a ring, the inner circle representing the raw or presocial organism and the outer the socialized organism. At infancy the outer ring is a thin and tender membrane; by mid-childhood it has grown thicker and tougher, into a kind of rind. By adulthood the inner aspect has been radically reduced and the outer socialized element dominates. By the time full adulthood is reached, let us say by the age of forty, the presocial part of the personality has been reduced to a small, recalcitrant remnant of what it was. Indeed, by that time it may be virtually impossible to identify anything but the socialized part of personality in the average person. A unique personal element in the personality will nonetheless always be present, for reasons which I will specify later. But it is a furtive thing, so much so that the individual may no longer even know what secret, elusive peculiarities he continues to harbor.

In dotage, when organic decay has taken its toll, when the boundary between the inner and the outer ring begins to dissolve or perforate, when the social program which society has so resolutely injected into the organism loses its form, or accumulates the insoluble residue of traumatic or unusual experiences, the personality may revert to what we sometimes call a second childhood. It may reclaim, in a melancholy pathological sense, some of the obstinacies of childhood. The pampering that was once devoted with such hope to the child becomes the despondent task of ministering to declining powers.

There is a common distinction in the literature on the growth and dynamics of personality, known generally as Self versus Other. Ortega y Gasset has written a splendid essay on the topic,[5] and it is found, too, in Søren Kierkegaard's brilliant and vertiginous *The Sickness Unto Death.*[6] It is fundamental to the social psychology of George Herbert Mead, upon whose ideas I will draw liberally here.[7] The Self-Other distinction is now a commonplace in sociology, psychology and psychiatry. It is, nevertheless, still useful.

The core of personality, that bundle of organic, largely hereditary dispositions—the infant with its need to be nursed, fondled, protected, its need to kick and squirm and experience itself—is the basis of what comes to be the Self. It is a subjective thing, what we think of when we use the word "I," personality felt from the inside. But such an "I" is its own kind of abstraction. From inception, the organism is inextricably, hopelessly, irrevocably bound up in a network of environmental forces, sights, sounds, odors and symbols, and it is only for convenience's sake that we think of the "I" as skin-contained. We do so because we carry the center of the world with us everywhere we go. "I" and our body processes become the same thing.

As the individual experiences the world around him, as the infant learns that it is wiser to bite the blanket than to bite its toe, the blur between Self and Other begins to dissipate. When it finds that it is more rewarding to bite the blanket than its mother's nipple, the distinction grows clearer. In systems jargon, what is taking place during the development of Self is establishment of a communication loop between the personality and the external situation. Information flows between the infant and its mother, later between the infant and others, sisters, brothers, father, teachers and playmates. The world is its task-environment and so personality becomes a cultural strategy.

95

This development of Self-Other distinctions depends upon the rewards and punishments experienced. But until the process has proceeded for some time, the child continues to display egoistic, "I"-centered behavior—if you like, selfishness.

However, it is such conditioning that makes the learning of the rules of the social game possible. Thus internalized rules make up the social self. George Mead called this social self "Me," intending to emphasize its reflexive quality. For simplicity's sake, we can refer to the two parts of the personality as Self and Reflected Self. The Reflected Self is rather like Charles Cooley's "looking-glass self." [8] It has properties in common with Sigmund Freud's Superego, the Id-Ego being roughly equivalent to what I call the raw Self. I do not wish to get tangled up in jargon. The process by which the personality becomes a reflection of what society expects it to be is the essential point here.

The social programming of the raw organism so that it can live in society is not haphazard. It involves building a complex internal mosaic of response potentials. They are assembled in packets, as definitions of appropriate role capabilities. These "rules active in us"—to use Peirce's definition of a habit—tell us how to behave as "brother," "sister," "warrior," "waiter," "flunky," "ambassador," "chaplain," "champion," as well as "goat." They also prescribe how we are to behave in complex collective Self-Other relationships, relations as members of the laity toward a class called "priests," for example, or "followers" in a leader-mob relationship—this can be pretty chaotic—or "citizen" in relationship to "nation."

The basic unit of society, however, is the duet in which we participate with the Other. The more general the nature of the Other, the broader the social universal we must construct to deal with it; "the nation," for example, when we think of ourselves as "citizens." Such construction of social rules takes place, when it is not a jerry-built thing, according to the logic governing inductive inference. The truth-use of our opinions about the Other, therefore, determines our success in playing the social game. It is also a measure of the success of society in making individuals into members of its cast of players.

As socialization proceeds, the external loop between Self and Other is gradually internalized, learned. It is copied as an I-Me relationship. The internal loop becomes an "analogue of the external situation"—to refer again to Tustin's phrase— a psychological record of a sociological relation. That is why Jivaros agree about headhunting, why Mormons think like other Mormons, why members of a nation feel something in common.

The development of an internal psychological isomorph of the external social situation is the foundation of self-awareness. This awareness is reflected in the very roots of our language. We speak of "myself" or "ourselves." We "talk to ourselves." We mutter to that other person we see in the bathroom mirror as we shave. We soothe, upbraid and commiserate with that other being as we lie awake in the dark. We damn him for his failings, praise him for his achievements, even give him credit where none is due. But it is this dialogue that permits us to "see ourselves as others see us"—to the extent that we can—to tell right from wrong, to feel guilt, responsibility, virtue, sinfulness, mortification as well as pride.

"Thought," observes George Mead, "is inner conversation." This is very much to the point. Our thoughts can, in fact, be detected in minute vibrations of the vocal cords. In fact, "thinking" is correlated with many minute unobservable physiological movements and changes in muscle tone.[9] Speech and thought are in that sense, again, isomorphically related. Hence, too, the importance of Benjamin Whorf's hypothesis about the significance of language in the way we think about the world.

But it is the internal conversation that makes introspection possible, lays the foundation for an I-Thou dialogue, provides us with consciousness, since full consciousness at the human level is not simply sentiency but self-consciousness.

But while it is true that such consciousness has a long phylogenetic history, that mere sentiency is different from full consciousness (which is why Socrates could ask whether it is better to be a happy pig or an unhappy man), it is not an either-or situation. We cannot assume that animals lack self-consciousness even if it is apparent that they have much less of it than we do. If one argues that only man has self-consciousness, the retort is obvious. Which man do we mean? Pithecanthropus? Australopithecus? Do we only include scholars who write on the subject? The growth of self-consciousness is, however, reflected in what we call insight, the capacity to "think things over," to "take stock of ourselves," to ask questions such as "What came over me?," to feel embarrassment, to see the tragic and reach for the heroic.

Actually, the term "insight" could be reversed. It might be called "outsight," since what we must do when we try to develop it is to get outside ourselves so that we may look back in. We must not only feel ourselves as subjects but experience ourselves as objects. We compliment the person who is able to do this by calling him "objective." The fact that many people do not develop insight to the full is why certain people utterly lack a sense of humor, why so many of us take ourselves too seriously, why, too, there are those pathetic fellows who do not know when they are being insulted. According to what I have said here, such persons are really not fully conscious.

The curious habit of so many people today to respond to queries by saying that they "feel" so-and-so rather than "think" such-and-such is, again, evidence of the peculiarly subjective quality of present-day life, as well as its regressive nature. For while thinking requires a dialogue between the Self and the Reflected Self, feeling does not. Feeling is a simpler thing than thinking. This is not to say that many men cannot think too much. They do, and intuition remains a potent thing. Certainly our intuition tells us that much is wrong in the world today that thinking does not appear able to put right.

The Self-Reflected Self internal communication loop is a record of social experience, but its actual neurological properties remain very much a mystery. We have some clues as to what it might involve from studies that treat some brain functions as analogues of environment feedback,[10] and computer simulation of the processes of concept formation provides clues.[11] But the critical function of the internal Self-Reflected Self loop, as far as individual adaptation is concerned, is that it is a predictor system, and personality, so interpreted, is a strategy. If it is a poor predictor, as with the neurotic or psychotic, it brings psychological defeat upon itself for the same reason. Just as the correspondence between single opinions and reality determines the truth-use of these opinions, correspondence between personality and Other will measure the truth-use of personality. 167120

If we visualize the individual in an increasingly complex social field with, say, four participant Others, we can imagine how segments of the outer ring of the personality, Reflected Self, are linked to reciprocals. If a small boy is surrounded by father, mother, sister and teacher, each one of these external relations is a loop, a feedback circuit, along which positive and negative signals flow. These external loops define many of his habits and become "rules active in him." They instruct him how to behave in various social situations. As a sequence of roles is played, it is as if the ring of the social self rotated, each rule notched into it triggering a response from another person. Roles depend, then, upon shared information and, as is obvious perhaps, the development of human languages enormously expands the capacity of society to store information in roles. It simultaneously increases complexity of personality structure.

The function of social conditioning is to produce predictable behavior in predictable situations, to activate social rules which the individual can gradually broaden to larger and more complex classes of social experience. An ideal society would be a totally predictable society perfectly matching an equally predictable environment. Since no such environment exists, theories of society unavoidably become theories of social change, theories of adaptability of individuals in collectivities.

If we think of our Self image as what we think we are, and our Reflected Self image as what we think others think we are, we can measure the personality's need to change as the tension between the two. If we wish to make the equation more complex, we can then ask questions of what others think we think they think we are, *ad infinitum*. To reduce the tension between his Self image and his Reflected Self image to optimal levels, which is not the same as trying to eliminate it altogether, the individual has several options—some superficial, others bearing a closer relation to the essence of self. The individual can change his opinion of himself, or he can attempt to get others to change their opinion of him. The first option can be painful. It may require apologies and amends, new sets of New Year's resolutions, admissions that we have made asses of ourselves. It may involve a surrender of identity, the replacement of a something we know by a something we do not, a possibility, a self by a yet-to-be self. It is not strange that even the neurotic will cling tenaciously to a maimed self rather than take chances with what he might become if he were to change.

The second option can cost as much. It may require enormous effort to try to convince others that we are different from what they think we are. It may force us to risk the substitution of a wholly personal definition of being for one that is defined wholly by the social. Tillich examines this sort of Self-Other problem at a deeper, existential level in his examination of *The Courage To Be*[12]—in the one instance, the courage to be "as oneself," and in the other, the courage "to participate," to become "as a part," for example, "as a part" in "democratic conformism." Basically such problems come down to the simultaneous need to hold on to sufficient consciousness to maintain one's identity and to draw upon the bank of experience which society makes available in the Other. In the one case, there is the threat of loss of awareness; in the other, the threat of loss of meaning. Nietzsche says somewhere that "the function of the will is to maintain consciousness." Consciousness, then, declines as we are ruled by habit, the acts prescribed by roles within the Other. Hence, the greater the gamble as we simultaneously attempt to be "as oneself" and "as a part." Hence, too, Kierkegaard's formula:

> The more consciousness, the more self; the more consciousness, the more will, the more will the more self. A man who has no will at all is no self; the more will he has, the more consciousness of self he has also.[13]

It is when I feel that what I think I am is different from what I think the world, the Other, thinks I am—or, if you like, to pursue the regress, what I think the Other thinks I think I am—that there is a motive for personality change. Change is related to the dialectic tension between Self and Other. It depends, that is, on doubt. But because information is banked more abundantly in the group than in the individual, more abundantly in "Me" than in "I," the pressure to conform over the long run outweighs our will to resist it. Induction is on the side of the group, not the individual. The courage to "be oneself" requires a gamble of will against heavy odds.

These distinctions between Self and Reflected Self become more blurred the more social rules active in us overlap, conflict or commingle. The "quiet desperation" in most lives is the struggle to maintain unity of our Self image under stress of role conflict. Stress within the personality can be raised to intolerable levels by immersing the individual in marginal positions between conflicting roles, between loyalties to family and loyalties to political beliefs, between a commitment to a marriage and the rules of an affair, between the force of received opinion in a professional group and contrary private conviction. The "marginal man" of sociological literature—the mulatto, the factory foreman, the second-generation American—experiences such stress. It can become especially intense when physical appearance conflicts with role, as it may, for example, among American Indian school-age children. If they look "Indian" but try to act "white," or if they look "white" and try to act as other "Indian"-appearing members of their family do, the stress may be extreme.[14]

Pathologies of the internal I-Me dialogue can take many forms. I noted several mild malfunctions as they may affect our sense of humor or capacity to feel embarrassment. But they take more subtle and damaging form during self-deception, the phenomenon to which so much existential literature is devoted. Jean Paul Sartre says, for instance, that the difference between a liar and a self-deceiver is that the liar is able to keep himself distinct from the object of his lying, and thus he remains conscious of his falsehood. During self-deception, a conspiracy between the "I" and the "Me" builds and the Self-Other distinction collapses. The Self learns to pretend that it cannot recognize what the Reflected Self expects of it. The Self closes its eyes to the mirror before it, or insists that it likes what it sees, that the nose is not as big as all that, that the eyes are really rather more beautiful than had been thought, that the profile is quite heroic in the proper light. The result of the self-deception conspiracy is a lowering of consciousness—indeed, the disowning of part of the personality—and its reduction to a thing that cannot make its relentless demands upon our probity. When the individual "gives himself" to a cause, on the other hand, he reduces his consciousness in the same way.

The process of self-deception, as Sartre points out in *Existential Psychoanalysis* and as Kierkegaard illustrates in the essay "Shadowgraphs," [15] is never a static thing. It is a continuous game of hide-and-seek, an endless regress of facing and eluding what one sees. This means that the "unconscious," as we ordinarily understand the term, to describe what we are unaware of and hence not responsible for, is itself self-deceptive. For, as Sartre insists, a psychological censor must know what to censor if it is to be able to censor. Self-deception is always something rather perverse, something rather deliberate, like a lie, a conspiracy against Self, against consciousness—a sin against the Holy Spirit, as theologians put it, by its very nature unforgivable.

For whatever comfort it may provide, one should note that in his essay "A Question to the Single One" Martin Buber exposes Kierkegaard's own curious self-deception; for example, in his vow of celibacy. Buber demonstrates the universal vulnerability to self-deception, how each of us is caught between what we think we are and what we think others think we are. Still, Kierkegaard is perhaps the greatest of all students of self-deception. Something similar was true of Goethe, and Ortega y Gasset has given us a stunning analysis of Goethe in self-deception: his failure, for all his genius, to come to grips with his own identity.[16] As for Sartre, need one do more today than point to his double-standard political logic?

The capacity of a personality to respond effectively to its task, to maintain predictive strength, is, to a good extent, determined by the speed with which information flows between it and its environment. What happens when this flow is blocked takes many forms in human events, as I have noted repeatedly. Additional illustrations are useful here. Upon learning of his defeat by Charles XII of Sweden at the battle of Narva, Peter the Great ordered the messenger to be strangled. Toward the end of World War II, Hitler increasingly greeted bad news in a rather similar way, as did Stalin. All organizations, in fact, face the problem of communicating bad news. When only good news is welcome, subordinates quickly adjust by turning sycophant, and while the leader preens himself, disparity between what he thinks and what others think may build to explosive proportions. His first realization that something is seriously wrong may come with his arrest and summary execution.

To some degree, all of us have problems facing unpleasant facts, and we may develop dangerous delusions to avoid the pain of doing so. Actual physical damage can bring on such problems quite abruptly. Damage to hearing, for example, may lead to paranoid delusions. That delusions can be lethal is illustrated by the case some years ago of Mbah Suro, the communist leader who died in battle with government troops in Blora, Java. According to the press reports, "Suro—who claimed magic powers to make men bulletproof—was shot dead in battle."

Self-deception is a pathology of the Single One, and as such is frequently associated with what I have called the romantic point of view. The reasons are that self-deception is more difficult to maintain on a collective than on an individual level. In the large group there is greater tendency for the deception to break down, and when the situation is extreme the truth survives underground. This does not mean that collective self-deception does not happen. It is possible for whole peoples to deceive themselves, to hide behind public opinion, seeking safety in numbers. The bigotry that masked as "fine old traditions" in the American South, traditions neither fine nor old, is an illustration; so, too, the self-righteous, sentimental liberal. But group self-deception is more like a lie. There are always whispers in the coffeehouses that betray public self-awareness. To the solitary individual, however, such whispers must come from within. Each man must be his own censor.

Study of the pathologies of the internal dialogue could occupy an entire book. Still, two dimensions of such pathologies deserve special comment here. Harry Harlow's studies of infant monkeys isolated from birth from all social contact indicate that one result of such deprivation is failure of the organism to develop Self-Other distinctions. When frightened, for instance, highly self-destructive behavior may replace normally defensive responses. The animal's teeth must sometimes be extracted to prevent self-inflicted injury. In later life, these creatures display a range of social pathologies, inability to mate, inability to relate socially. They refuse to accept their young or they display excessive attachment to them.[17] Moreover, much of this damage appears to be irreversible.

In humans, failure to distinguish Self from Other can be observed in more common, innocuous forms as well as in extreme pathologies. A youngster may pull his hair when a parent frustrates him; we scratch our head when faced with a puzzle or kick the footstool instead of our wife. But we may also commit suicide. An object within the Self replaces the external Other.

Many vital psychological qualities of individuality are related to development of the Self-Other distinction. The individual's capacity to give as well as to accept love, his capacity to develop altruistic attitudes and to identify with others, are shaped by early experiences which determine rules active in the Self–Reflected Self relationship. Affect hunger, a simultaneous craving for affection and inability to accept or provide it, seems to relate to such early experiences within the family constellation. Also, certain forms of homosexuality are evidently forms of irreversible role programming established in the child during periods of hormonal plasticity. Thus far, at any rate, chemotherapeutic and social-psychiatric methods can "cure" only a very limited number of such cases.[18] Normal sexual response potentials must evidently be fixed by appropriate role experiences while the organism is chemically receptive to such modeling. The effects of early deprivation, to which I alluded earlier, are consistent with this evidence of the relative irreversibility of many human fixations and complexes.

Satisfactory personal adjustment depends upon our opportunity to maintain a healthy set of role experiences over time, and this role repertory must be exercised if it is to stay healthy. We can witness what happens to the individual when he does not have such opportunity, or when sudden shock, such as the death of a mate, deprives him of it abruptly. Managed sensory deprivation—e.g., solitary confinement—can dissolve the individual's Self image by destroying the established I-Me communication circuits within the individual. Corrections practices have often relied on this principle in attempting to regenerate criminal personality. During the late nineteenth century, the State Penitentiary of Philadelphia isolated its inmates so that they could ponder the evils of their ways, presumably allowing the antisocial personality to decay. It was assumed that in isolation criminal habits atrophy for want of reinforcement. A new program of socially acceptable habits could then develop spontaneously under pressure of God-given conscience. Similar principles are implicit in more sophisticated modern sensory deprivation technology. Extreme stress, torture, enforced sleeplessness, systematic social cue-mixing, scrambling rewards and punishments, and so on, are used to tear down the old personality, "brainwashing" its social program out of it. The individual is then submerged in a new set of experiences, new rewards and punishments that insure absorption of a new Self image.

Natural forms of social deprivation can occur when the death of a partner in a marriage of long standing occurs, or when job retirement is forced. These experiences can cause substantial psychological disorientation. In geriatric psychiatry there is considerable evidence that sudden or clumsy removal of an aged person from a family group can have devastating physiological consequences, effects that are often more pronounced than direct physical injury.

In many psychiatric methods, the operating principles are similar. The "neurosis" or "psychosis" is lessened by psychoanalysis, chemotherapy or manipulation of reinforcers, as the case may be. Alleviation and "cure" of mental disease, indeed, is sometimes treated as equivalent to reduction of observable deviate behavior; e.g., in anorexia.[19] The management of the external social situation can have powerful curative influence on the internal psychophysical condition of the individual.

This is all consistent with interpretation of the Self–Reflected Self dialogue within the personality as an "analogue of the external situation," such as I outlined earlier. It is also consistent, however, with what we know of the increasing importance of internuncial tissue, tissue that performs the comparator function in our body's data processing, during the evolution of animal life. One neuropsychological definition of a voluntary act says that its key is the capacity for "continually changing selective responsiveness" to new experience.[20] The function of the internal loop between "I" and "Me," or the Self and the Reflected Self, is to allow the personality to correct its actions in social mid-flight, to guide the individual in its adaptive responses as it moves toward a goal by drawing upon a repertory of a continually accumulating bank of experience. Such behavior is purposive or teleological, because it is basically a negative feedback system.

At each new point in time, the personality is a combination of the deposit of past experience and the social situation of the moment. The record of the past is, for the most part, a deposit mixed with situational experience all our life long. It is a coadunation, and since time runs in but one direction—in our world, at least—the product is inevitably unique. It never can be fully duplicated. Unlike role, which is always a class of acts enclosed by the rules of social inference, "I" stands outside such rules. This is a profoundly important point if one is to consider the nature of leadership and at the same time take into account the arguments of the modern behaviorists.

The historically unique quality of personality has been essentially missed by the behaviorists. They cannot deal, even within a probability framework, with acts that are distinctive, for their very rarity makes such acts unpredictable. This is why the attempts of the behaviorists to deal with the concepts of freedom, dignity and evil are so mechanistic and clumsy. By insisting upon his predictability, they transform man into a mere object in a situation. In the fullest sense, theirs is "now" thinking. B. F. Skinner's bewildered interpretation of Dostoevsky illustrates this odd, self-imposed helplessness of the hyperrationalist attempting to deal with moral issues. The full existential significance of the question "Who shall decide?" simply evades him.[21]

Leadership is always something unique in that "to lead" is

to create. To be a leader means that one chooses to be a creature of will and consciousness, not the projection of a social curve. That is why "opportunity" is so critical a thing in the life of the Great Man. For opportunity is chance, and chance is a remorseless thing, an abrasive that erodes structure and certitude from collective life and leaves us with the free particles of indeterminacy. Chance, time and will are thus allies. For even in a world solidified by rules, put together slowly by the Sisyphus labors of the life force, stone upon stone, a sliver of chance is all that is necessary to preserve a remnant of opportunity.

THE TINCTURE OF SOCIOPATHY

The organizational Great Man has much in common with the artistic Great Man, and much has recently been written on the subject. Most of research indicates a relatively consistent set of traits, both in science and in art.[22] The creative personality, for one thing—no surprise perhaps—is somewhat more intelligent, as measured by traditional I.Q. examinations, than the average person, though there are startling exceptions. However, he seems to display a higher degree of imagination and divergent intelligence than the person with equally high traditional convergent intelligent skills. He enjoys complexity more than the less creative individual, and he has greater skill at metaphoric thinking. He has a freer temperament, seeming to prefer feeling to judging. He is more candid toward his body functions and is more willing to talk about them than is the less creative person. He has a capacity to establish remote associations between events, and can disassemble and reassemble experience in a freer way than the ordinary person. There also seems to be a degree of paranoia and hypochondriasis associated with many of these people. These latter traits are probably related to the creative personality's heightened sense of personal life history, which, in turn, may be related to the self-conscious sense of destiny often evident in the Great Man. More important, this sense of calling often acts as a positive feedback influence on an individual's imagination and drive. It produces an autarchic fantasy and the conviction that one is free to go beyond limits of behavior set for ordinary people.

The autarchic fantasy has a sociopathic tincture. It is often very apparent in the Great Man. He sets himself outside the social rules of ordinary men if only to have his way in society. He does not make, nor could he make, a complete break with the society around him. It is, after all, the means to his ends. Thus, Alexander the Great saw nothing inconsistent in setting himself above ordinary men even as he worked among them. These seemingly conflicting requirements can take a humorous twist. When told by his commander Parmenio that he must not go to battle in May because it was unlucky by Macedonian tradition, Alexander merely suggested that the name of the month be changed. But consider what the historian Allan Nevins has to say of Henry Ford:

> The dreamer, the man of intuitive mind, is usually an artist, and many puzzling contradictions, even many repugnant acts in Ford, become comprehensible if we think of him as essentially a man of artistic temperament. His detachment, his arch, wry humor, his constant self-projection into the spotlight, his ability to lift himself above business minutiae, his readiness to do some terrible things with . . . little seeming consciousness of their quality . . . all suggest an artistic bent.

Ford, adds Nevins, "hit upon truths by divination, not ratiocination," and, quoting biographer Dean Marquis, he adds that Ford "had a different view from other men of what was possible and impossible." [23]

Despite what I have said about the Great Man's readiness to "do some terrible things," there is nonetheless evidence that leaders who are successful for long periods of time read the social situation around them more accurately than does the average follower. And when this is not the case—and it was not with Ford—the organization which the Great Man assembles may suffer severely for this inadequacy. But both small group studies and participant-observer studies of gang leadership indicate that the leader is usually a better judge of social reality than followers.[24]

There is a striking paradox involved here. K. E. Read describes it well in a study of leadership among the Gahuku Gama of New Guinea. I must quote Read at length, since the elements that parallel Nevins's comments on Ford are so apparent:

> A man who seeks influence and desires to gather followers must exhibit the qualities and possess the skills which convey the ideal of "strength." Indeed, his overt behavior will conform quite closely to the stereotype of the "strong" man. He will behave assertively and with swagger. He will exhibit a strong *awareness of his individuality,* a sense of self-importance; and he will act as though he expects others to follow. Yet at the same time, he must acknowledge and espouse the ideal of "equivalence." Among other things, this means that although in some measure he must attempt to dominate others, he must also recognize their right to parity. . . .
>
> These qualities and skills suggest a man who is endowed with a high degree of *self-consciousness.* . . . Apparently it is necessary for him to place a judicious emphasis on self-interest, and in turn this seems to imply some *conscious manipulation of the basic values.*
>
> So I have heard some of the more respected leaders describe themselves as "bad men." . . . In describing themselves as "bad," it seems to me more likely that these men

are expressing their awareness of the antithesis between "strength" and "equivalence." There is a manifest tension or inconsistency between these ideals. . . .[25] [Emphasis mine.]

It is the sense of freedom from the rules which govern ordinary men, the tincture of sociopathy, that gives the Great Man the freedom we see at work in messianic behavior. It is this sense of freedom that permits an Adolf Hitler to proclaim that he and he alone "will act for Germany," for a Boss Hague to declare "I am the law," for a Roosevelt to try to pack the Supreme Court during an American time of trouble.

In some accounts of the political career of Roosevelt, the traits that I have said are associated in the Great Man syndrome stand out so clearly that one has the feeling that he himself was a student of the subject, which he was not. When he was "in unfamiliar territory," he had the conviction that "he could do no wrong." There are his occasional slips indicating that "his mood was one of imperialistic Realpolitik rather than idealistic imperialism"; airy suggestions that incompatible ideas could best be dealt with by having his subordinates "weave the two together"; his remark in the campaign of 1936 that "There's one issue . . . it's myself, and people must be either for or against me." [26] And then there is also his notorious confidence in the power of his own charm over such formidable individuals as Stalin.

Anthony Storr's study of Churchill's personality fairly bristles with descriptions of traits forming the Great Man syndrome. There are "prolonged and recurrent fits of depression," which Churchill called the "Black Dog"; evidence that he was a "man who was, to a marked extent, forcing himself to go against his own inner nature"; an extraordinary reliance on intuition—that "keen nose for things in the bud pregnant with future possibilities" of which Jung speaks in describing the intuitive personality type. There is a heedlessness toward the feelings of those around him; a curious, almost infantile inability to realize that he was "not the center of the universe"; a powerful need to demonstrate physical courage and, with it all, a great gift of wit and oratory. Storr suggests that much of Churchill can be explained by an affect hunger which stems from his experiences as a child, so that "at a deep internal level" he felt "himself to be predominantly bad." [27] But note in particular the significance of historicity in the dynamics of the will of Churchill. Here is not the hollow ping-pong ball that behaviorists make of man, or indeed the dreary abstraction the social sciences would give us as a replacement for man.

Most of the psychological traits that seem critical to the Great Man syndrome appear to be traits that are established in the personality at an early age. There is little evidence that these traits can be trained or educated into an adult human by such crude devices as creativity training, sensitivity sessions or psychotherapy. There is even less evidence to suggest that democratic attitudes—other than in the sense of Gahuku Gama "equivalence"—are associated with the syndrome. Quite the reverse would seem to be so. There is a subtle, authoritarian, conscious management of basic values. Such violations of the basic value system, indeed, often identify precisely the deviate quality of the Great Man. Then, too, certain abnormal physical traits may add to the appeal of the deviate. Medicine men among some primitive tribes are recruited from among epileptics, on the assumption that the seizures are a supernatural credential. Certainly in a case such as that of Joan of Arc it was helpful to hear voices.

Another interesting behavior of the Great Man is what Arnold Toynbee calls the pattern of "withdrawal and return"; of Jesus' retreat to the desert for forty days and forty nights of fasting and contemplation, for example.[28] The same behavior is common in eminent contemporary political leaders.

The intense demands for public behavior at one period seem to require solitude at another. The phasic pattern involved resembles Hans Selye's stress cycle. It is as though conscious search behavior in the Great Man requires isolation, at Berchtesgaden or Colombey-les-deux-Églises, temporary withdrawal from society and its confining rules of the public game.

One of the intriguing elements in leadership deviance is the intuitive grasp of the historical qualities of situations in which the Great Man finds himself. The self-image of such men, especially as it is reflected in their insight, sometimes has a highly ironic quality, as if it were the only way heightened insight into the human condition could be borne. The sense of irony reflects the capacity to see the contradictory nature of being a "bad" man. It was that curious quality in Roosevelt that allowed him to joke about the precise number of captured Nazis that would have to be killed in order to get Stalin to agree to work more amicably with Churchill.[29]

Most men will not, of course, take another man seriously if that man does not take himself seriously. The Great Man appreciates this and usually avoids irreverent public wit. While he may cultivate a deadly serious public style, however, he may disguise his insight into the tragicomic nature of what he is about by refracting it through an ironic humor that his followers really do not grasp. On the other hand, it is often also true that the Great Man will so submerge himself in his role that this ironic quality is entirely suppressed. As organizations institutionalize, in fact, this is more and more necessary of their leadership. Leaders who have given themselves entirely to the ritualized requirements of their role will thus turn to cant and platitude in place of fire and brimstone. If one is to be treated as a sacred cow, one must learn to act like one. As leadership institutionalizes, qualities that connote stable, solid and predictable performance, such as a stuffy bearing, become proportionately more important. Such a bearing is particularly important in structured situations such as appearances before committees on finance. A stuffy humorless person projects a mood of sanctity into the situation; the wisecrack is out of order. Established organizations, after all, operate at a lower level of consciousness than do organizations in process of formation, and wit can puncture the reverence required of their ceremonial events.

Some interesting elements of this syndrome come to light when we examine the temperamental traits of the Great Man as a romantic. The basic premise of the romantic's view of the world, according to Hulme, is that human nature is good and that the cause of man's woes lies in the oppressions of society. The non-romantic, the classicist, sees man quite the opposite, as a highly culpable creature, from which something decent can be gotten only by social regulation. "To the romantic, man's nature is like a well, to the classicist more like a bucket." [30] While we have all encountered exceptions to this rule, shallow wells and deep buckets, the essential thing about the romantic is that the road to virtue, goodness, truth and beauty is a retreat from social regulation; that is, regressive behavior. The tincture of sociopathy in the "bad man" is one of the traits that enable him to regress and, when necessary, to junk a habit when the price of harmony becomes too great.

Several of the temperamental qualities associated with the romantic also appear in the Great Man of art. Victor Lowenfeld has made a distinction, for example, between what he calls haptic and visual orientations to the world.[31] In the haptic personality, the individual's image of the world is built from a subjective base, whereas the visual personality begins with the environment and constructs his image of the world the other way around. Interestingly enough, the distinction seems to hold good even when the visual individual is physically blind. But this haptic-visual distinction is rather like the introvert-extrovert distinction, and it also parallels the distinction which one psychiatrist makes between octophils and philobats.[32] The first is a person who psychologically clings to the object world about him, adjusting to it as though he were climbing a tree, relinquishing his hold on one element of experience only as he gets a firm grip on another. The philobat, on the other hand, is the kind of person who meets uncertainty in a thrill-seeking, daredevil style, tightrope-walking his way through the world. Both types are presumably ambivalent toward the world, one being suspicious, mistrusting and critical, the other acting superior and condescending. Something similar distinguishes men of ecstasy and "men of excellence." The man of ecstasy joins in Henry Miller's haptic cry, "Do anything if only it produces joy. Do anything if only it yields ecstasy."[33] The man of excellence, on the other hand, is the person for whom, in Ortega's words, "life has no savour unless it be in service to something transcendental."[34]

For help in identifying what that transcendental principle would be, I think we may well turn once again to Peirce. The principle is what we have traditionally called altruism, which is defined in most dictionaries as a regard for, and devotion to, the interest of others. But the root of the principle is not merely sentiment but logic and will. Peirce says that a logical man should not be selfish because

> Death makes the number of risks, or our inferences, finite, and so makes their mean result uncertain . . . [and thus] we are driven to this . . . our interest shall not stop at our fate, but embrace the whole community.[35]

The paradox of such a logic of love is that its source of energy lies in the individual, and this energy must be converted from an empathic impulse to an altruistic rule. Moreover, it must be a conscious act if it is to be a transcendental act, a commitment and not merely an effect following upon a cause. It is the consciousness of such an act, its will, that enables the individual to transcend his own fate. For while the roots of collective well-being lie in the subsoil of personal need, the bloom, altruism, survives and spreads its reach only in the light of social concern.

VI

TOWARD A
STEADY-STATE
IDEOLOGY

FOR CENTURIES, the progress culture has made a virtual fetish of change. Whole libraries sing praises to the value of it. Schools exhort the young to seek and enjoy it, and the public media warn the old of the danger of not keeping up with the times. This presents a particularly mean problem to the progress culture, because making a fetish of change becomes a form of resistance to change itself. For the fact is that there is no inherent value in change for its own sake, and while nothing in the universe remains forever unchanged, the degree of desirable change for any living system changes. The value of change lies entirely in the contribution it makes to adaptation and survival, and this always depends upon cost. If the environment is relatively stable, a living system, once it is well adapted, need change little to maintain itself. If the environment is uncertain, the opposite is true. Self-induced need to change, however, is something else, as I noted earlier in commenting on the behavior of positive feedback processes. Such change can decrease rather than increase the margin of survival, and it then becomes pathological. It becomes self-destructive, like a serpent devouring its tail. This is the present condition of the progress ideology. It has become a self-destructive dogma.

The honeybee has some profound lessons for us about change. His order of life, Hymenoptera, has been on the earth a great deal longer than man, and long before humans appeared the honeybee was a master designer, aviator and social engineer. He has also built some very impressive societies. Only within recent decades have we begun to appreciate fully just how impressive they can be. Karl von Frisch is perhaps the most renowned student of the honeybee, and it was he who first discovered how the insect communicates vital information about the location and quality of nectar and pollen sources for the manufacture of honey and wax.[1] He found at the same time a most impressive illustration of how an insect community balances the need for change against the need not to change.

Frisch found that among certain species of bees information about the location of nectar sources is reported by scouts by a dance they perform within the hive on the vertical surface of the honeycomb. It takes the form of a flattened figure eight. The triangular relationship between the comb, the sun and the flower bed is transcribed onto the comb, so that the axis of the figure eight relative to the top of the comb, which is treated as the fixed position of the sun, becomes a direction finder. We have in a honeybee community, then, a fascinating cybernetic model. Scouts perform a scanning function in the system; the dance serves a memory function that banks the long experience of the hive in exploration and energy exploitation; the ferrying worker bees perform the appropriate labor in the changing environment. But what is of special interest here is that only about 88 percent of the workers in the community follow instructions provided by the dance. The remainder deviate in varying degrees from the dance's instructions—for whatever reason, error, genetic delegation, venturesome spirit, stupidity or sociopathy (depending on how closely one identifies with honeybees)—and it is the deviate minority that brings in information about new sources of nectar and assures that the community will not commit itself fatally to an unchanging response to the environment. However, since not all scouts return with valuable new information, survival of such communities depends upon a careful match between the cost of subsidized exploration and the benefits of the majority's conformity to instructions of the dance. It is a constant problem of balancing deviation and conformity, a constant "Contest Between Harmony and Invention," as Antonio Vivaldi might have called it. Such contests are universal in nature, and we should therefore now look more closely at what creativity, invention and innovation involve.

ADAPTIVE DEVIATION

Ever since the Romantic era, when special virtue was imputed to being rustic and uncouth, the progress culture has inclined to think of creativity, especially in the arts, as a mysterious gift lodged among the repugnant habits of odd people. And certainly it is clear that many artists have lived disordered, tormented and driven lives. So, too, with many great political leaders, messianic figures and assorted varieties of genius. Albert Ryder, the American painter, lived a recluse existence in rooms crammed with rubbish, soiled clothes and dirty dishes. Contemporary painters, such as Arshile Gorky and Nicholas de Staël, committed suicide. Thomas Edison worked with almost demonic fervor, and Guiseppe Verdi remained intensely creative even as a very old man, composing *Othello* when he was seventy-four and *Falstaff* when he was eighty. On the other hand, Jean Sibelius and Frank Lloyd Wright were anything but classic bohemians, both notorious dressers, whereas Piet Mondrian and Wassily Kandinsky were inclined to go about looking as ordinary as the next shopkeeper. Certainly the Japanese and Dutch cultures make it obvious that there is no clear correlation between creative output and being dirty, hairy or pungent, fashionable as that belief may be today.

Creation involves two elements: the deviate or mutant act and its validation. The nature of validation varies, and it may be years in following the creative act itself. Gregor Mendel's discoveries in genetics are a famous illustration of just how long it may take for such validation to occur. But the function of a creative act derives from its problem-solving strength, whether we consider it as a process of molecular assemblage,[2] the reduction of psychological tension—e.g., Churchill's "Black Dog"—or playing a social role with exceptional skill and daring, as in the Great Man. But I would hold that the problem-solving nature of creativity is as true for Pablo Picasso painting *Three Musicians* as it is for Cyrus McCormick inventing the reaper, as true for Sibelius at work on *Tapiola* as it is for a traffic engineer inventing a solution to highway congestion, and that it is also so with chimpanzees meeting a new threat in their jungle home or a weaverbird assembling its nest under unusually difficult conditions.

Very little is known about the real nature of the aesthetic impulse in either man or the other creatures. There is some evidence that the bowerbird, for instance, has a kind of aesthetic impulse.[3] It is probable that as more is learned about the other animals we will grant them more and more the benefit of the doubt, or at least stop putting down some of what appears to be their aesthetic sense as "mere" instinct. It is also probable that as we do we will better come to understand why humans have the curious habit of erecting elaborate rules in arts and sports only so that they can struggle to circumvent them. The pleasure we get in doing so, and the delight we take in graceful mastery of difficult problems, is probably related to the sense of confidence that goes with the economic use of our energies in meeting challenge. But why an appreciation of the beautiful should be an evolutionary advantage is certainly not clear, though it may be that forms in nature become beautiful as they approach ideal functional form, and vice versa. D'Arcy Thompson's remarkable studies of form in nature have such an eerie Platonic implication about them. Nature seems to be trying somehow to reveal the ineffable to us by holding us spellbound within its architectonic wonders.[4]

In a famous little book called *How We Think,* published in 1910, John Dewey outlined what he believed to be the basic phases of the problem-solving process. It begins with a perplexed, troubled or confused situation and ends with a unified, settled or resolved situation.[5] He broke these two phases into five more specific elements: a "felt difficulty," a recognition of the difficulty as a "problem," production of tentative solutions, some "mental elaboration" of them, and finally a test of one or another such solution in imagination or action.[6] Thus thinking is a test in imagination, deferred action.

Dewey took the essentials of these ideas from Peirce; *How We Think* is an enlargement of the ideas which Peirce had published much earlier in such essays as "How to Make Our Ideas Clear." Such a phrase as "felt difficulty," for example, which became popular in progressive education, is a paraphrase of Peirce's "irritation of doubt." Nonetheless, many writers have followed Dewey's energetic lead in the study of the problem-solving process. One writer speaks, for example, of phases of preparation, incubation, illumination and verification;[7] another refers to a process of "general assessment," "broader functional solutions" and selection.[8] And Herbert Simon, to whom I alluded earlier, notes three phases of problem-solving in organizational behavior: intelligence—in the military sense of the word—followed by design and choice.[9]

The three-phase structure of problem-solving is implicit in a wide range of organic and social adaptive responses: in theories of physiological stress,[10] in theories of perception,[11] in theories of types of intelligence[12] and in stages of cultural revitalization.[13] The basic structure of the problem-solving process involves (1) an initial period during which the sensory equipment of the system, its receptor or input apparatus—whether individual or group—is opened to new or troublesome experience; (2) a period of scanning, during which alternative explanations are sought and compared with past experience; and (3) a final stage in which a solution is selected. It is an open-scan-close sequence. Since this sequence is continuous in living systems, we should think of it coiling through time, with a feedback loop linking each sequence of responses.

The term "set" has often been applied to factors which limit the scanning capacity of the organism. Traditionally the term has a strong negative overtone—getting into a rut being considered in the progress culture especially heinous. Set, however, is really just an attempt to solve new problems with old solutions, and it is based on inductive inference, prediction. If we view it, as Hebb does, as "selective attention," [14] its value depending upon its cost-benefits as a predictor, it loses much of its negative connotation. A fixed narrow attention range consumes less energy than a wide attention range, and it is this economy that makes a habit useful and, in fact, explains why social roles and traditions develop.

There is evidence that many psychological control-reducing factors can be helpful to the creative scanning process. Just what is involved neurologically is not clear. But we do know that Samuel Coleridge's famed unfinished *Kubla Khan* came to him after he awoke from a heavy dose of opium. He mentally completed some three hundred lines before a bill collector interrupted his creative episode and forced him to accompany him to town. He had put down fifty-four lines. When he returned to his desk, he was unable to recall any of the remaining lines, and the work remains a fragment.

Alcohol can sometimes also serve to reduce psychological control, and the drinking habits of writers have often been commented upon in this connection, though it is far from clear that creativity is improved directly by drinking. But there is little doubt that drinking can have at least a temporarily dilating influence on the scanning process. Herodotus notes that one of the means by which Persian military leadership generated a large number of tactical alternatives was to discuss them while "warm with wine." They selected from among these alternatives the following day when the sober light of dawn lent things a less expansive cast. Thus, it is said, they "combined boldness with caution."

Fatigue apparently can have comparable effects on the creative nonconscious assemblage processes. The history of discovery and creative composition contains many illustrations. The discovery of methods for isolation of insulin by Frederick Banting is said to have come to him when he awoke at two o'clock in the morning after a long and exhausting day studying diabetes. The closed-chain theory of the constitution of benzene is said to have struck its discoverer, August Kekulé von Stradonitz, while he was drowsing in front of his fireplace. And Mrs. Julia Howe composed the immortal lines of the "Battle Hymn of the Republic" before dawn after she awoke from fitful sleep. An appreciation of the value of reading the nonconscious for clues to conscious life also motivated the American Indian to practice vision quest. The individual isolated himself for prolonged periods of fasting in order to induce hallucinations that he could then interpret as a guide to life. Indeed, it is this quest for a guide to life that motivates many of the seemingly pointless excesses of the drug culture among the youth of today. But on the importance of the role of the nonconscious in self-renewal Emerson noted that "sleep takes off the costume of circumstances, arms us with terrible freedom, so that every will rushes to a deed. A skillful man reads his dreams for his self-knowledge." It scarcely need be added that psychoanalysts have repeatedly made the same point.

Though here and there in the literature we have autobiographical comments on conscious control of set-breaking, it is something that few creative personalities have been able to articulate. I know of no more succinct statement on the subject than Frank Lloyd Wright's essay "The Concept and the Plan." The open-scan-close sequence is obvious in his description of conscious management of imagination, especially the capacity to break set. I will quote him at some length:

. . . Conceive the buildings in imagination, not first on paper but in the mind, thoroughly, before touching paper. Let the buildings, living in imagination, develop gradually, taking more and more definite form before committing it to the drafting board. When the thing sufficiently lives for you then start to plan it with instruments, not before. To draw during the conception or sketch, as we say, experimenting with practical adjustments to scale, is well enough if the concept is clear enough to be firmly held meantime. But it is best always thus to cultivate the imagination from within. . . .

If original concept is lost as the drawing proceeds, throw all away and begin afresh. *To throw away a concept entirely to make way for a fresh one,* that is a faculty of the mind not easily cultivated. Few architects have that capacity. It is perhaps a gift, but may be attained by practice. What I am trying to express is the fact that the plan is the gist of all truly creative matter and must gradually mature as such.[15] [Emphasis mine.]

As for throwing away concepts, Sibelius makes this remarkable observation about the need to be able to let go of a creative product that the artist knows is not quite right:

> Greater success makes one more and more prone to scorn solutions that come too easily, that follow the line of least resistance. . . . The thing that has pleased me the most is that I have been able to reject. The greatest labor I have expended, perhaps, was on works that have never been completed.[16]

Deliberate engineering of set-breaking behavior—the conscious design of situations that insure a broadened range of selective attention, a greater degree of search—is still poorly understood. One primitive device in vogue a few years ago was so-called "brainstorming," sessions in which groups were asked to generate as many ideas as possible without regard, at the moment, for quality of ideas. There is undoubtedly some validity to the idea that social pressures in a group situation tend to force conformity on the individual and to reduce scanning. Several classic sociological studies of norm formation demonstrated this point years ago.[17] It is moreover evident that reducing threat can increase scanning freedom of intellectuals in large institutions. But there is also evidence that a single individual can brainstorm as successfully in solitude as he does in a group. Letting pedestrian personalities loose in a brainstorming session probably does little more than make for more pedestrian talk. Certainly the evidence that we have about the creative habits of such persons as Gustav Mahler or Paul Cézanne makes it pretty clear that great artistic achievement is not necessarily a public process.

Varieties of organizational designs and devices have also

developed in industry and government that are intended to increase the scanning capacity of groups. The so-called "think tank" is one, and theoretically at least it is supposed to reward search and scanning and to censure closed-mindedness. Universities, too, have for centuries supposedly been designed to maximize scanning or search behavior, providing such devices as tenure to protect the free thinker. Unfortunately, most organizational systems of any duration tend strongly toward bureaucratization simply as the force of circumstances, cost and a need for harmony press upon them. To underscore the point, I need scarcely mention the mountain of literature, systematic studies of "bureaupathologies," [18] as well as novels portraying the incredible lengths to which the bureaucratic mentality will go to suffocate creativity. Hyperrationality, with its inherent tendency to reward specialization, has the same depressive effect upon creativity. In fact, the very essence of hyperrationality is analytic, not synthetic, and it is inevitably anti-creative. It splits experience into pieces rather than putting it together in configurations. This is why hyperrationality and bureaucratization are such natural allies and why they reinforce each other so spontaneously in driving institutions toward predictability and control and away from freedom and flexibility. It is one of the special paradoxes of managed organizations in a hyperrational progress culture that while they must survive in a world of uncertainty and often intense natural competition, they offer on the one hand—the opportunity to invent, what they withhold on the other—the demand for harmony.

If one takes a culturological view of cultural problem-solving, it becomes immediately evident that the open-scan-close sequence also occurs as a collective process but that the single individual, the historicity of individual personality, comes into play in a most pronounced manner during the scanning part of the sequence. One cannot read Edward Gibbon, Oswald Spengler or Brooks Adams,[19] for example, without being impressed by the fact that while the rise and fall of cultures is a collective process, there are periods within the process when the key consideration is the historicity of Great Men, messiahs and leaders. They are found to perform the same function in a culture attempting to adapt to trying circumstances as Frisch's deviate bees. The terrible danger of social set, cultural selective attention, also becomes clear, since it often blocks incremental change and forces tensions to build to the point of a major social crisis. This is what is now happening in the progress culture, and it does not bode well.

Anthony Wallace has given us a particularly useful description of the problem-solving sequence at work in cultural events in his studies of revitalization movements. Since he pays a good deal of attention to the role of messiahs in such movements, I think it is useful to sketch some of what he says.[20] Wallace indicates that revitalization movements move through a series of relatively distinct phases: a beginning period in which relative stability prevails, a second phase in which stress develops, a third in which collective stress reaches intolerable levels and a fourth in which spokesmen for a new order, a new social equilibrium or steady-state condition, come forward. As one or the other "solution" is selected and wins acceptance, social life once again passes under the rule of institutional forms and the need for other messiahs declines.

The first stage is a condition of dynamic equilibrium between the culture and its environment. The culture is meeting the needs of its people; stress is limited and tensions tolerable. God is in his heaven, the priests are at their altars, the barns are full and tables are piled high with plenty. The everyday things of life are well in hand.

The rise of stress within the culture, the second state of the process, comes on imperceptibly. Little by little, the mesh between institutional parts of the culture worsens and the culture becomes a less reliable analogue of the external environment.* Its predictive value and adaptive capacity begin to decline. There is a rising level of moral conflict in the system as the difference between what people do and what they profess increases. The gap between the most frequent behavior and the most desirable behavior increases. One of the error signals which appear, in other words, is social hypocrisy.

The third phase of the process is what Wallace calls a period of "cultural distortion." It is an exacerbated version of the second phase. The culture increasingly fails to satisfy basic needs. A heightened level of public anxiety develops and expresses itself in a whole range of collective responses resembling those of a psychiatrically disturbed individual. Romanticized interpretations of the "good old days" may appear alongside the most rancid cynicism—Adolf Hitler proclaiming, "When I hear Wagner, it seems to me I hear rhythms of a bygone world," even as he engineers the most craven butchery. There may be frantic efforts to manufacture instant tradition, such as the Nazi use of the swastika, a symbol of ancient gods of war. Or there may be frantic efforts to infuse banal political pronouncements such as *Mein Kampf,* or Mao's "little red book," with mystic force and significance. Scapegoating responses are also frequent, directed, as the case may be, at Jews, capitalists, revisionists or anarchists. Subversives are seen peering through every potted palm. A variety of withdrawal responses also occur, isolationist foreign policies, or bohemian movements based on half-baked interpretations of

---

* It should be emphasized that what is meant here by the "external situation" is any condition of the task outside the system visualized in the abstract. Political corruption, for example, may occur within a society, yet remain external to other parts of the "system."

Asiatic thought. In other words, the era is marked by wild oscillation in public mood and sentiment and by compulsive hunt behavior. Fads follow upon fads, cults displace movements, movements revert to fads. The period is characterized by doubt, doubt representing, as Peirce put it so well, not a habit but "privation of a habit." [21] The decay of old ways strips individuals of social guidance and exposes them to the hazards of solitary values.

A great many conditions can bring on such a time of troubles. Basic climatic change can affect agriculture and means of basic subsistence. Agricultural methods may exhaust the soil, forcing the whole system toward imbalance and decline. Such appears to have happened, for instance, in the decline of the great Mayan cultures of the Yucatán Peninsula. Or populations may rise and increase pressure on food supply. Famine may set every man's hand against every other man's in a primitive struggle to survive the day. Or epidemics may sweep the land, or mass unemployment. Military defeat can cause the collapse of a political regime and tear the rudder from public institutions. Or technological change—industrialization, for instance—can upset the relationship of classes; scientific discoveries can sever the religious moorings of social values. The result may be a series of shock waves, stress, tension, collisions or civil war.

During such periods, there is often an oversupply of "solutions" available, and it is during such a time that every kind of self-elected leader, messiah, quack and Great Man may come forward with his solution to the problem. When Hitler came to power, for example, there were monarchists, social democrats, communists, fascists and hosts of splinter groups vying for power, each in its own way illustrating the abundant supply of ideas being thrown up by the times as possible solutions to German problems. The Nazi regime, as it turned out, lasted only twelve years and proved a deadly social evolutionary sport. But its defeat turned upon a series of quite incredible chance events, and one can only speculate what the world would be like had, for instance, Hitler's regime developed an atomic weapon ahead of the Allies.

A notable aspect of periods of intense cultural scanning during a period of cultural distortion, as Wallace calls it, is that broad institutional patterns of habit tend to loosen or break up, so that the system settles from a collective to a more individualized manner of action.* Smaller and more flexible social groups thus become the seedbed for messiahs. This is why messiahs appear first as gang leaders, and why so often, as Wallace notes, the group's new beliefs form around the personal experiences of a single individual, many of which may be hallucinatory in nature. John Wesley led such a movement, as did the Mahdi in the Sudan. And among the American Indians there was Handsome Lake's movement among the Seneca in 1799, the Delaware prophet during Pontiac's uprising against the British in 1762, the Shawnee prophet and Tecumseh movement of 1805. It is not accidental, of course, that our own black civil rights movement should produce its Martin Luther King and its Malcolm X. I would stress the personal quality of such experiences, since, again, it is this historicity that provides the mutant idea that is needed during

---

* The revitalization sequence evidently has a sufficiently clear wavelike pattern to allow sigmoidal curves to be applied to them. F. S. Chapin describes this as a three-part "societal reaction pattern." (See F. S. Chapin, *Cultural Change* [Dubuque, Iowa: William C. Brown Co., 1928], chaps. 7–8.)

Such curves seem to apply to many cultural growth forms; e.g., to the evolution of Mayan sculpture from an archaic period through a flamboyant middle period to a final decadent period. (See Tatiana Proskouriakoff, *A Study of Classic Maya Sculpture,* Publication 593 [Washington: Carnegie Institution, 1950].)

a cultural time of troubles. This is often called genius. But, as Jean Paul Sartre says, genius is "not a gift but the way one invents in desperate cases." [22] The desperate case is the cradle of what I have been calling the Great Man. It could as well be said of great ideas. But it is resistance to the insights of genius that often brings on the desperate case itself, and when this resistance brings on a crisis natural correctives also come into play. They are often more cruel than a tyrannical genius. They are also often tragic because a great idea that might have delivered the culture from its trials was spurned at the time it was most needed.

NATURAL CORRECTIVES

A quantum collapse in the conditions of human life on the planet is now a real and ominous possibility. It is this possibility that stirs such deep anxiety in the modern mind. It is not the death of God Nietzsche announced ninety years ago as much as the death of our secular substitute for God, our belief in endless materialistic progress, that fills us with chill and foreboding. Not only are we being forced to accept a radical change in our view of man's primacy in nature, a view that says we are more dependent upon such lowly creatures as plankton and earthworms than they on us, but we are being forced to concede that with each day that goes by the operation of grim natural correctives to our intoxication with the idea of progress becomes more certain. We are being forced to concede that such ideas as those of Thomas Malthus, who described over a hundred and seventy years ago what would happen if human population overreached its resources, were not merely gloomy formulations that progress has made look ridiculous. Progress only hastened the day of reckoning with what he said, and we now see man like an animal caged in a planetary zoo. As man reaches the limits of his living space, he begins to sink into the smear and mire of his own waste. Just as a colony of bacteria multiplying in a petri dish reaches the limit of its space—and toxic waste controls further growth by depressing the colony's chemical environment, forcing the organism to retreat to a condition of cystic torpor—the present rate of human population growth is forcing such a retreat upon the progress culture. When, for instance, millions of gallons of fish-killing phosphate sludge were accidentally released into the Peace River in Florida, it meant not merely the destruction of a seafood industry; it meant partial destruction of the culture that allows such eco-atrocities to take place. When the brains of children are irreversibly damaged by lead-paint poisoning, it is not just their brains that are damaged but the culture that boasts of "better living through chemistry." And when scientists are driven by perverse curiosity to produce test-tube babies, it is not merely the compulsion that is involved but the larger pathology of a hyperrational culture that permits such things. All across the front of the progress culture's major institutions, in other words, natural correctives come more and more intensively into play with each new excess. The point to be borne in mind is that these are spontaneous reactions, and only in part, if at all, conscious or rational in origin. The operation of natural correctives is therefore often violent and unsparing, great natural oscillations of too much and too little. But they are the result of fixation, an overcommitment to some idea or usage which may have worked for a while but is suddenly bankrupt in the face of new conditions. Historians such as Arnold Toynbee talk at length about this sort of thing; for instance, how the Spartans fixated on the phalanx formation in warfare until bested by the Theban column, which, in turn, was unable to cope with

Macedonian formations of skirmishers, phalangite and cavalry.[23]

The story of the Aztec response to Spanish invasion is especially dramatic as an illustration of cultural inflexibility in face of threat. The Aztec might have easily overwhelmed the Spanish—at least in initial confrontations—by sheer force of numbers had they not persisted in interpreting capture of victims for religious sacrifice as the primary motive in fighting. But equally impressive is the way in which Montezuma clung to interpretations of his dreams as evidence of certain doom before the invaders.[24] The idea of progress holds us transfixed in the same way. Many of us would rather perish than surrender the dream. The twin gods of fortune hover over all such events: willingness to use the past, and courage to break with it when necessary.

The price of inflexibility in institutions is especially stark during war. In war, the price of mistakes is high and the consequences all too obvious—sunken ships and corpses on the plain. These, too, are natural correctives. I would illustrate the price for cultural set, therefore, by noting several remarkable illustrations from military history. A particularly fascinating illustration concerns the events at Yorktown in 1781, which proved so decisive in the American Revolution. At the time, General Cornwallis was trapped at Yorktown by a land force of French and Americans and a French fleet of some twenty ships, under Admiral de Grasse, lying in the Chesapeake. At the same time, the British had a comparable fleet of nineteen ships at New York under Admiral Graves. It was sent to the Chesapeake to try to assist Cornwallis by sea.

During the years preceding these events, training of officers in the British Navy was strongly influenced by what were known as *Rooke's Fighting Instructions,* a body of tactical rules considered to be the distilled wisdom of British naval experience. For reasons which are themselves a classic study in bureaucratization of problem-solving, the rules ultimately became known as *Rooke's Permanent Fighting Instructions.*[25] But among its cardinal instructions was a rule against breaking "line formation" during an encounter. Squadrons were taken into action with van, center and rear squadrons in line formation, and the enemy was engaged by broadside fire.

The effects of the rule upon Graves's tactics at Yorktown are notable. As he sailed south toward Cape Henry and caught de Grasse at anchor, the Frenchman weighed anchor and made a desperate scramble for the open sea. Graves brought his fleet into the bay, came about in classic line formation, attempting as best he could to get de Grasse's disorderly fleet into the appropriate conterminous line formation. Instead of falling upon single elements of the French fleet as they came up, destroying them almost at leisure, Graves actually hove to at one point in frantic search for the orthodox arrangements with which the disorganized enemy could not accommodate him. It was as though Rooke's instructions had neglected to indicate what a commander should do when enemy squadrons did not line up. De Grasse escaped to sea. At sea, his fleet was more than a match for his opponent. Graves retired to New York for repairs; the noose tightened around Cornwallis, and he was forced to capitulate. The line-ahead fixation, born in 1691, was not broken until 1783. It prevented, according to one British naval historian, a "wholehearted defeat upon any enemy in any stand-up fight" for about ninety years.[26] A point we should keep in mind here is that when Rooke's instructions became "permanent," the behavior they ruled regressed to a lower level of consciousness than they occupied during the time that they were being developed. An equally vivid case is described by Robert Bruce in his *Lincoln and the Tools of War*. It involves a remarkable

135

memorandum of June, 1861, from one Colonel (later General) James W. Ripley, then Chief of Ordnance:

> A great evil now specially prevalent in regard to arms for the military service is the vast variety of the new inventions, each having, of course, its advocates, insisting on the superiority of his favourite arm over all others and urging its adoption by the Government. The influence thus exercised has already introduced into the service many kinds and calibers of arms, some, in my opinion, unfit for use as military weapons, and none as good as the U.S. musket, producing confusion in the manufacture, the issue, and the use of ammunition, and very injurious to the efficiency of troops. This evil can only be stopped by positively refusing to answer any requisitions for or propositions to sell new and untried arms, and steadily adhering to the rule of uniformity of arms for all troops of the same kind, such as cavalry, artillery, infantry.[27]

Even when an inventor complied with the elaborate regulations designed to foil him, "Ripley usually refused to make tests, whether a model was supplied or not, without a direct order from his superiors—which generally meant President Lincoln." This policy blocked the large-scale use early in the war of repeating rifles. Their use might have had an early decisive influence on the course of the conflict.

But there are some arguments for Ripley's position, and his memorandum is not actually as stupid as it appears to be. He did not know how long the war would last, and major changes in weaponry involved complication and disruption of production and training techniques, and perhaps a series of modifications in support methods. His was a question of judging the need for harmony as against the price of invention.

There are more recent and bloody illustrations of the price of military set. During the first months of World War I, French commanders insisted that infantry wear red pantaloons as a symbol of *élan,* and they refused to use the machine gun because it was considered a defensive, cowardly weapon.[28] Thousands of these colorful warriors had to be killed before natural selection forced the use of field-gray uniforms more suited to the soldier living in the trenches with rats or on his belly in the mud. In World War II, the Germans quickly adapted their famed "88," originally designed as an anti-aircraft weapon, to the needs of tank warfare in North Africa. The British had a similar anti-aircraft weapon, somewhat larger than—some authorities believe superior to—the "88." For obscure reasons, it was never used as an answer to the German gun.

More interesting for what it says about institutional set is Corelli Barnett's account of the difficulties which the British Army had in attempting to use infantry, artillery and tanks as coordinated units.[29] Tank units—the descendants of horse cavalry—were usually led by officers drawn from British social strata different from those which infantry and artillery officers were drawn from. The result was a curious inability to weld coordinated units from the three services. The Germans, perhaps because they loved war more than they cared about social class, had no such problem. But as a comment on social form and war, probably no incident is quite as impressive as one that occurred during the fall of Singapore to the Japanese: "Even on the eve of Singapore's surrender, a British gunnery officer was told he needed permission from the golf club committee before he could mount guns on the links." [30]

Such illustrations lead us into another complex of problems in the resistance of social systems to change; namely, the tendency for the specialist to use his expertise to perpetuate "permanent fighting instructions." A quotation from Winston Churchill to Lloyd George on the convoy crisis of 1917 makes the point nicely.

No story of the Great War is more remarkable or more full of guidance for the future than this. It was a long, intense struggle between amateur politicians, thrown by democratic parliamentary institutions to the head of affairs, on the one hand, and the competent, trained, experienced experts of the Admiralty and the great sea officers on the other. The astonishing fact is that the politicians were right, and that the Admiralty authorities were wrong. The politicians were right upon a technical, professional question ostensibly quite outside their sphere, and the Admiralty authorities were wrong upon what was, after all, the heart and centre of their peculiar job. . . . The firmly-inculcated doctrine that an admiral's opinion was more likely to be right than a captain's, and a captain's than a commander's, did not hold good when questions entirely novel in character, requiring keen and bold minds unhampered by long routine, were under debate.[31]

Inasmuch as I discussed the problem of institutional set in the knowledge industries at length in an earlier chapter, I will not enlarge much here upon the way in which the "great sea officers" of the professions—medicine, psychiatry, sociology and such—perpetuate the permanent fighting instructions of the progress culture. But there are numerous illustrations that come readily to mind. In mental health, for example, organizations may pursue harmony by the invention of problems, so that:

There is a peculiar circularity of the supply-demand function in the area of mental hygiene. . . . As more therapists are trained, demand for their conversation increases.[32]

Similarly, one of the implications of psychiatric studies in Manhattan seems to be that a goodly percentage of the people living on the island are in need of psychiatric care.[33] To be sure, this is the usual assessment of the out-of-town visitor who experiences the city's crosstown traffic, hostile hotelmen

138

and the choleric worker population. But the definition of a large percentage of Manhattan's population as mentally ill is doubtlessly reassuring to mental health professionals working there. It also indicates why evidence that "talking therapies" have little measurable impact should be less than welcome in the profession and why evidence pointing in the opposite direction, which is that talking therapy may reinforce and prolong illness, should be considered heresy.[34] The talking therapies do not suffer in face of negative evidence, but thrive. The same is true in mental health social work graduate school training. The schools of social work devote themselves intently to the elaboration of more graduate degree programs, despite data indicating the weakness of such curricula. I recently participated in reporting information that indicates that when social workers take Master's degrees their actual effectiveness in day-to-day service declines rather than improves. They mimic long-discredited psychoanalytic practices, become office-bound and surround themselves with increasingly abstruse and artificial professional vocabularies.[35]

Such responses also suggest how specialized vocabularies help insure professional survival. While it is evident that much specialist vocabulary in the sciences and technology is unavoidable, erection of abstruse jargon and pedantry, especially in the social sciences, is really analogous in function to the lid on the burrow of the mud wasp. It can be opened only from the inside. It is not surprising, therefore, that efforts to simplify problems—for instance, in psychiatry—by organic rather than functional approaches to illness elicit resistance. In psychiatry, the direction of scientific thinking has been steadily toward removal of illness from the functional category,[36] and there is no doubt that chemotherapy has had profound influence on our thinking about the nature of emotional illness. Nevertheless the mere suggestion that schizophrenia, for example, may involve blood factors or genetic determinants can elicit panic and resentment among social scientists committed to sociological theories of the disease's cause. While it comes as no surprise to anyone who has ever had to take an aspirin the better to survive a long staff meeting, the suggestion that man's social responses are linked to his organic being, his social life to his physical state, is not infrequently taken as an affront to sound sociological thinking. By insisting that such psychic problems are really social in origin, that is, they are claimed as the special province of social science. There is nothing particularly unique about such responses. Professionals adapt, after all, like members of any other species, be they limpets or tickbirds, by carving out and defending a specialty among a throng of competitors. Everyone must make a living. But it should be observed that in each case "progress" tends to be equated with multiplication of professionals, not solution of the problems to which it is supposedly addressed.

Resistance to conceptual flexibility among specialists, however, is one of the prices we pay for harmony among them. But insofar as harmony draws upon rigid selective attention and the idea of progress represents such selective attention, it focuses thinking upon immediate survival. It blinds the specialist to long-range problems and, by lulling him into the happy opinion that the future will inevitably be better than the present, becomes a detrimental illusion. It pits expertise against foresight and by doing so produces the deformed offspring of rationalism I have called the hyperrationalist.

One of the compelling things to observe in the present response of the progress culture to its problems is the way it clings ever more desperately to its illusions, covers its face with its hands whenever its crimes are revealed to it and surrenders itself to the force of natural correctives. Consciousness of our predicament seems in many cases only to add to our need to avoid facing reality. It does not, as one would expect, were we as rational as we claim to be, cause us to turn resolutely to the task before us. We shrink from our duties to ourselves, like an addict terrified of the pain of withdrawal. Our new ecological awareness has had this effect among many of us. The reason is doubtlessly the added pain that such awareness brings. Aldo Leopold noted this when he once observed:

> One of the penalties of an ecological education is that one lives alone in a world of wounds. Much of the damage inflicted on land is invisible to laymen.[37]

And so it is as evidence increases of the destructive environmental effects of pesticides, plastics, airborne cadmium, nickel, lead and displacement of oil with underground salt water. Such awareness generates in the business and technological community its own form of the retreat from consciousness. True believers come forward with the assurance that "what technology has wrought, it can undo," [38] ignoring the fact that technology is what technology has done. A deep, basic change, at its very roots, where our beliefs about what is good and what is not reside, would make technology something wholly different from what it is. It would cease to exist as we know it. For we are faced with the kind of thinking that moved whaling industrialists to insist that extinction of the sperm whale was unavoidable because some of its oils were irreplaceable in certain modern lubricants. And now the dolphin is being ground up for equally necessary reasons, so that the tuna-fishing technology can remain efficient. Madness, to be sure, but then so is exploration of Mars even as our institutions for the retarded, aged and orphaned remain disgusting pits of filth and neglect.

But evidence of an impending abrupt and spontaneous loss

of faith in technology and its underlying progress precepts can be seen almost daily in the public media. One recent dramatic illustration was Delaware's decision to limit further industrialization of its bay coast.[39] The decision stunned many progress ideologists and left federal officials in the Department of Commerce bewildered and bitter, complaining that the state should not take such action in the face of economic losses, as though these losses were simply a matter of superficial business and industrial arithmetic, as though again one could eat with the devil by merely lengthening the spoon. The same bewilderment surrounds such well-intentioned, if erratic, efforts as that of Denver to outlaw urban problems by limiting in-migration to the city. Much of the backlash against "eco-freaks," in fact, is motivated by the anxiety to which increasingly visible ecological wounds expose the ordinary man.

The squalor of large cities, the breakdown of big-city educational systems, the rise of counter-culture and the rest are natural, nonconscious, though cruel, responses to a danger, like the rise of an inflamed pustule when infection occurs. We must appreciate that when such natural correctives come into play they are often only superficially self-conscious responses to our culture's difficulties. Indeed, many of our seemingly deliberate responses to our present problems are not really conscious in the full sense of the word at all. Slogans such as "the New Federalism" and "citizen participation" are at once cognitively empty and intuitively correct, because they betray much deeper forces at work than the rhetoric leads us to assume. "Participative democracy" and "citizen participation," for example, at heart mean clumsy decentralization, regression of political controls of representative government. It does not actually mean that the poor, the illiterate, the helpless and the imprisoned have seized, or been given, conscious control over their lives. It means that power is decentralizing and that natural correctives are asserting themselves because the consciously designed system of social management cannot carry the load put upon it by the progress culture. Mobs cannot govern themselves any more than the Chinese Cultural Revolution was governed by the throngs milling about in city squares insulting one another with posters. This sort of "participation" is but a prelude to severe, often bloody, regimentation.

There is unfortunately very limited evidence that we shall be able to take the measured steps required to ease ourselves down from the perilous place to which progress thinking has laid so glittering a path. We seem capable of only the most modest ameliorative responses—distribution of birth control pamphlets, some improvement of automobile exhaust systems, cleaning a small river here and there, more talk of returnable beer bottles. Barry Commoner is correct in welcoming even these efforts, and applauding citizen efforts to mount more serious and far-reaching programs to control waste and senseless "progress." But the treacherous turn that technology has taken with the invention of pesticides, non-biodegradable plastics and such, which Commoner discusses so well in a chapter entitled "The Technological Flaw," is more than a flaw.[40] A basic and profoundly powerful dynamism is in trouble, and the heart of that dynamism is the belief in endless material progress. So we may anticipate a bewildered and panic-ridden immediate future and a series of frantic and largely ineffectual responses to our problems. We may also expect increasing sympathy for abrupt totalitarian solutions. There will be talk of *coups d'état*. Many of the ingredients of a *coup* are already here: a decline of public confidence in traditional democratic procedures as a way of solving problems, growing alienation of the military from civilian values—an all-volunteer army will intensify it by further isolating the military from civilian values—and the increasing frequency of major eco-disasters. Such events not only increase the demands of the public to "Do something!" They also make it increasingly difficult to work deliberate, thoughtful and fundamental change in economic, political and social thinking that rests on progress thinking. If a *coup* takes place, it will in a way be a vicious natural corrective. In times of trouble, men turn spontaneously toward praetorian rather than pacific values.

A FINAL NOTE ON RATIONAL SOLUTIONS

To some, much of what I have said about the progress culture will seem pointless pessimism. Yet I do not think pessimism and alarm should be confused. If we do not share Thor Heyerdahl's disgust at finding the mid-Atlantic covered by man-made filth, or Jacques-Yves Cousteau's shock at seeing sea life decline abruptly during his lifetime, or recoil at Jacques Piccard's warning that the oceans may be virtually dead in twenty years, we are fools, not mere optimists. Or if Samuel Ordway is correct in noting that high grade copper resources will be largely gone in fifty years, and lead, zinc and tin before 1980, one need be no pessimist to predict with confidence that our present "quality of life" will decline abruptly and that the shock will send a shudder through the planet.[41]

Of course, despair is not a strategy, and resignation is a limp substitute for one. So I would outline here what will be necessary if we are to find the courage and wisdom to try to reason and work our way out of our present problems. For one thing, we shall, by some means or other, have to try to manage consciously world culture. This is a task so staggering in scope that it seems almost pointless even to mention the possibility. Yet it is the only alternative to placing ourselves at the mercy of natural correctives. That we are likely to succeed in consciously managing our way out of our problems is a slim possibility. Yet we have few other choices.

The basic design of a consciously managed world culture would be similar to what biologists call an eco-climax system.[42] A mature forest is such a system. After competing species have adjusted to one another, relative equilibrium develops in which energy flowing into and out of the system more or less balances. Selection of a world eco-climax state toward which we could consciously aim our use of energy and effort implies, of course, fearful ethical issues. The number of people permitted to live on the planet would need to be fixed and the amount of its resources that each could use would need to be determined. This poses problems of deciding what resources to limit first, as well as how they are to be used equitably. There are few men presently prepared to face such grim decisions. Yet it is obvious that the depletion of nonrenewable resources sets the limits on any cultural end-state we choose. Indeed, the radical qualitative cultural change that will occur when crucial nonrenewable resources are gone has the profoundest implications for any design of managed world culture.

If we are to control our future to any meaningful degree, we shall have to construct a new science—perhaps it should be called an art—that is systemic in conception and planetary in scope. Nothing except the barest rudiments of such thinking exists today, and those that do exist—for instance, Jay Forrester's *World Dynamics,* or *Global Systems Dynamics,* which is a set of papers by a range of authors concerned with global systems—are but crude reflections of the complexities we face.[43] Moreover, they are haunted by hyperrational values, and some proposals are simply more super-science.

There have been many efforts in recent years to build systems of social indicators that could help the public-policy maker find his way through the complexities of contemporary events. There have been world-wide cross-cultural surveys that have tried to determine how cultures and natural conditions are correlated.[44] There are indicator systems in economics, political science, education and public policy. All are disappointing, for one reason in particular. They are not assembled against a philosophic framework that might provide them a configurational sense and thus allow the values implicit to the use of any such set of indicators to come to the surface. More usual than not, there is a deliberate avoidance of these value issues and a tendency to seek safety in the weary old shibboleths of "science." The result is that when such indicators are put to use they reinforce mono-dimensional thinking and make matters worse rather than better. They become an extension of technological distortions and fixations.

We need at very least the kind of "ecological impact inventory" of which Barry Commoner speaks in order to get a more reliable economic estimate of just what things "cost" in our society, and we need political policy based on environmental considerations such as L. K. Caldwell has called for.[45] We also need the kind of perspective that is developing in cultural ecology.[46] "Modern" man can learn a very great deal indeed from primitive man about the realities of cultural adaptation and survival.

A major obstacle to systemic thinking about world culture is that it is by its very nature a severe threat to the basic values of progress thinking. For a managed world culture would not only need to control population and energy use, it would have to cut back, and even eliminate altogether, some of the efforts now most dear to the technological and scientific community. Yet I think it is obvious to more and more laymen that there is something bizarre, and plain nonsensical, about a culture that launches multibillion-dollar projects to build space shuttles when that same culture cannot shuttle its working population from their factories to their homes without extremely costly and ludicrous traffic jams. The public will eventually respond to this kind of preposterous situation by concluding that our modern-day "permanent fighting instructions" are madness and that the "great sea officers" of science and technology, those who would have us manufacture test-tube babies in an overpopulated world or reduce man to a coldly conditioned animal, are aberrant and dangerous.

Rationality itself, as ordinarily understood, and as I understand it, is something else. It is good sense and logic applied without ostentation. It is not that vainglorious hyperrational aberration that would make man a god and make God a fiction. It is not the pretension that destroys normal emotion by quantifying it and mocks human spiritual needs with a cocktail, a quip or a slide rule. It is not war computerized so that blood and horror are no longer visible to men in the war room. Nor is it those thieving, gluttonous habits of a consuming culture.

The building of a science, or art, of world cultural management requires a massive shift in our basic theory of contemporary education. We must build a new kind of natural philosophy, something that Aldo Leopold would have understood, the kind of education that Sir George Stapledon speaks of, in the posthumously published *Human Ecology,* when he says that "the object of education should be to coordinate all the functions of man. Nature's own method of integration should be the principle and habit." [47] The significance of this new view is that it makes education a mirror of the real world and rescues our thinking from the trap of hyperrational narcissism. It drives us out of the laboratory and into the real world

147

of sun, soil and rain. It forces us to abandon the adolescent make-believe of "now" living. It rewards man for dreaming yet reminds him of the inevitability of nightmares.

Unfortunately, it is precisely in those areas of social and psychological management where our knowledge is most reliable that the most frightening ethical issues are lodged. It does not require a high order of intelligence, or even low-order paranoia, to envision a future in which converge the behaviorism that Skinner espouses, or the brain-implantation science that Delgado celebrates, and the total computerized society of which Arthur Miller warns us.[48] It would produce a world that could only be the nether place of madmen. Even now, design of a total Soviet social control system is evidently well along toward completion at the Kiev Cybernetics Institute. So it seems that we must once again face the ancient issue of who shall rule, but we shall have to face it within a grimly hyperrational world. Huddling behind populist slogans solves nothing in such a predicament, and merely forces the collision of the hyperrational world and that governed by uncompromising natural correctives. If we are to discover a way out of our predicament, we must surely find a middle course and to do so we must surrender some of those vain and deceiving aspirations that the progress culture once gave us. Paradoxically this surrender may be the most revolutionary victory for reason of all.

Notes

CHAPTER I

1. Karl Jaspers, *Reason and Existenz* (New York: Noonday Press, 1955), p. 20.

2. Ludwig Wittgenstein, *Tractatus Logico-Philosophicus* (London: Routledge & Kegan Paul, 1922), p. 187.

3. Karl Jung, *Modern Man in Search of a Soul* (New York: Harcourt, Brace & Co., 1933), p. 209.

4. Thomas Blackburn, "Sensuous-Intellectual Complementarity in Science: Countercultural Epistemology Has Something to Contribute to the Science of Complex Systems," *Science* (June 4, 1971):1003–7.

5. Paul Shepard and Daniel McKinley, eds., *The Subversive Science* (Boston: Houghton Mifflin Co., 1957).

6. William W. Behrens, Dennis L. Meadows, Donella H. Meadows, Jorgen Randers, *The Limits to Growth* (New York: Universe Books, 1972).

7. Jung, *Modern Man*, p. 96.

CHAPTER II

1. Harry E. Barnes, *An Intellectual and Cultural History of the Western World* (New York: Reynal & Hitchcock, 1937), p. 840.

2. W. B. Gallie, *Peirce and Pragmatism* (Harmondsworth, England: Penguin Books, Pelican Books, 1952), p. 22.

3. Charles S. Peirce, *Chance, Love and Logic* (Magnolia, Mass.: Peter Smith, 1949), p. 53.

4. C. I. Lewis, "The Pragmatic Conception of the A Priori," in *Readings in Philosophical Analysis,* H. Feigl and W. Sellars, eds. (New York: Appleton-Century-Crofts, 1949), p. 294.

5. Hans Reichenbach, *Experience and Prediction* (Chicago: University of Chicago Press, 1939), p. 314.

6. Norton E. Long, "The Local Community as an Ecology of Games," *American Journal of Sociology,* 44 (November, 1958).

7. Walter Goerlitz, *History of the German General Staff* (New York: Praeger, 1953), p. 96.

8. Charles E. Lindblom, "The Science of 'Muddling Through,' " *Public Administration Review,* 19 (Spring, 1959):86.

9. Herbert Simon, *The New Science of Management Decision* (New York: Harper & Row, 1960), p. 6.

10. Edward M. Weyer, Jr., "How the Eskimo Uses His Environment," 1932, in *Societies Around the World,* ed. Irwin T. Sanders (New York: Dryden Press, 1953).

11. Arnold Tustin, *Feedback, Automatic Control, A Scientific American Book* (New York: Simon & Schuster, 1955), p. 23.

12. Norbert Wiener, *Cybernetics* (Cambridge, Mass.: M.I.T. Press, 1948). See also W. Ross Ashby, *An Introduction to Cybernetics* (New York: Wiley, 1963).

13. J. O. Wisdom, "The Hypothesis of Cybernetics," 1951, *British Journal for the Philosophy of Science in General Systems,* Yearbook of Society for Advancement of General Systems Theory, 1(1956):121.

14. Karl Deutsch, *The Nerves of Government,* Part II (New York: Free Press, 1963).

15. Peter H. Klopfer, *Behavioral Aspects of Ecology* (Englewood Cliffs, N.J.: Prentice-Hall, 1962), p. 28.

16. Arturo Rosenblueth and Norbert Wiener, "Purposeful and Non-Purposeful Behavior," *Philosophy of Science,* 17 (1950):318–26.
    See also C. W. Churchman and R. L. Ackoff, "Purposive Behavior and Cybernetics," *Social Forces,* 29(1950):32–39.
    See also Mary A. B. Brazier, "Neural Nets and the Integration of Behavior," *Perspectives in Neuropsychiatry,* ed. D. Richter (1950), H. K. Lewis Co., pp. 35–45.

17. Lauriston Sharp, "Technological Innovation and Culture Change: An Australian Case," *Cultural and Social Anthropology,* ed. Peter Hammond (New York: Macmillan, 1952), p. 93.

18. Donald R. Dudley, *A History of Cynicism* (London: Methuen & Co., 1937), p. 36.

19. Robert N. Linscott (ed.), *The Stories of Anton Tchekov* (New York: Modern Library, 1932), p. 173.

20. Kenneth Boulding, "Revolution and Development," in *Changing Perspectives on Man* (Chicago: University of Chicago Press, 1968), pp. 222–25.

21. Richard Hofstadter, *Social Darwinism in American Thought* (New York: Braziller, 1955).

22. John Dewey, *The Child and the Curriculum* and *School and Society* (Chicago: University of Chicago Press, 1902).

23. Joseph Morgenstern, "Twilight of the Booster," *Newsweek,* July 5, 1971, p. 9.

24. Wisdom, "Hypothesis of Cybernetics," p. 112.
    See also Wiener, *Cybernetics,* pp. 7–8.

25. Theodore Morgan, "The Theory of Error in Centrally

Directed Economic Systems," *Quarterly Journal of Economics* (August, 1964).

26. R. H. MacArthur, "Fluctuations of Animal Populations and a Measure of Community Stability," *Ecology,* 36(1955): 530–33.

27. Gregory Bateson, "Bali: The Value System of a Steady-State," in *Social Structure: Studies Presented to A. R. Radcliffe-Brown,* ed. Meyer Fortes (Oxford Clarendon Press, 1949), pp. 35–53.

28. Joseph Altman, *Organic Foundations of Animal Behavior,* (New York: Holt, Rinehart & Winston, 1966).

29. Leslie Reid, *The Sociology of Nature* (New York: Pelican Books, 1958).

30. Eugene P. Odum, *Fundamentals of Ecology* (Philadelphia: Saunders, 1959), chap. 7.

31. A. E. Treat, "The Reaction Time of Noctuid Moths to Ultrasonic Stimulation," *Journal of the New York Entomological Society* (1955), pp. 165–71.

32. Omar Khayyam Moore, "Divination—a New Perspective," *American Anthropologist,* 59, no. 1(February, 1957):69–74.

33. C. R. Carpenter, "Territoriality: A Review of Concepts and Problems," in *Behavior and Evolution,* Roe and Simpson, eds. (New Haven: Yale University Press, 1958).

34. Gaetano Mosca, *The Ruling Class* (New York: McGraw-Hill, 1939), p. 126.

35. Walter Lippmann, *The Public Philosophy* (New York: Mentor Press, 1955), pp. 123–38.

36. Garrett Hardin, "No One Dies of Overpopulation," editorial, *Science,* 172 (June 25, 1971), p. 1297.

37. John Calhoun, "Discussion on Promotion of Man," in *Global*

Systems Dynamics, ed. E. O. Attinger (New York: Wiley-Interscience, 1971), p. 63.

38. William M. Carley, "On the Defense," *Wall Street Journal,* November 30, 1970.
See also "Radar Wipes Out IRS Tapes," *Computerworld,* 4, no. 52(1970):1.

39. Arthur Miller, *The Assault on Privacy* (Ann Arbor: University of Michigan Press, 1971).

40. Charles H. Southwick and M. Rafiq and M. Farooq Siddigi, "Primate Populations and Biomedical Research," *Science,* 170, no. 3962 (December 4, 1970).

41. Philip M. Hauser, *World Population Problems,* Foreign Policy Association Headline Series, no. 174 (New York, 1965), pp. 7–9.

42. "The Trillion-Dollar Economy," *U.S. News & World Report,* February 9, 1970, p. 29.

43. Albert E. Burke, "Influence of Man Upon Nature—the Russian View: A Case Study," in *Man's Role in Changing the Face of the Earth,* ed. William L. Thomas, Jr. (Chicago: University of Chicago Press, 1970), 2:1036.

44. "Science Called Slave, Not Man's Master," *Milwaukee Journal,* Comment on the News, March 18, 1970.

45. "Scientist Raps NASA on 'Seeding' of Mars," *Milwaukee Journal,* November 16, 1970.

46. Melvin Small and J. David Singer, "Patterns in International Warfare, 1816–1965," *Annals of the American Academy of Political and Social Science,* 391:68.

CHAPTER III

1. Jerry Rubin, *Do It: A Revolutionary Manifesto* (New York: Simon & Schuster, 1970).

2. "Human Potential: The Revolution in Feeling," *Time,* November 9, 1970, pp. 54–58.

3. "The Sensuous Therapist," *Newsweek,* September 20, 1971, p. 66.

4. J. M. R. Delgado, *Physical Control of the Mind: Toward a Psychocivilized Society* (New York: Harper & Row, 1969), p. 88.
See also Leon R. Kass, "The New Biology: What Price Relieving Man's Estate," *Science,* 174, no. 4011 (November 19, 1971).

5. Reinhold Niebuhr, *The Children of Light and the Children of Darkness* (New York: Scribner, 1944), p. 17.

6. Stuart Chase, "Forty, Thirty, or Five Hours a Week," *New York Times Magazine,* May 30, 1954, p. 10.

7. "Peeling Back the Land for Coal," *Newsweek,* June 28, 1971, pp. 69–72.

8. Victor A. Thompson, *Decision Theory, Pure and Applied* (New York: General Learning Press, 1971), p. 16.

9. José Ortega y Gasset, *The Revolt of the Masses* (New York: Norton, 1930), p. 112.

10. U.S. Bureau of the Census, *Statistical Abstracts of the United States, 1968,* 89th ann. ed., p. 105.
See also U.S. Department of Health, Education and Welfare, *Projections of Educational Statistics to 1977–78,* 1968 ed.

11. Daniel P. Moynihan, "On Universal Higher Education" (53rd Annual Meeting of American Council on Education, St. Louis, Mo., October 8, 1970), pp. 25–35.

12. R. H. MacArthur, "Fluctuations of Animal Populations and a Measure of Community Stability," *Ecology,* 36 (1955): 530–33.

13. Bryce Nelson, "A Surplus of Scientists: The Job Market Is Tightening," *Science,* Vol. 166, no. 3905 (October 31, 1969): 582–84.

14. C. H. Townes, "Quantum Electronics and Surprise in Development of Technology," *Science,* 159 (February 16, 1968): 702.

15. Leslie A. White, *The Science of Culture* (New York: Straus & Co., 1949), p. 214.

16. Ruth Moore, "The Search for Mankind's Ancestry," in *Evolution of Man,* ed. Louis B. Young (New York: Oxford University Press, 1970), pp. 198–213.

17. James G. Miller, "The Individual as an Information Processing System," in *Information Storage and Neural Control,* William S. Fields and Walter Abbot, eds. (Springfield, Ill.: C. C. Thomas, 1963).

18. W. C. Allee, A. E. Emerson *et al., Principles of Animal Ecology* (Philadelphia: Saunders, 1960), pp. 350–52.

19. Thorstein Veblen, *The Higher Learning in America* (Stanford, Calif.: Academic Reprints, 1954), p. 176.

20. Daniel S. Greenberg, News and Comment, "Basic Research: Britain Tries to Measure Payoff," *Science,* 166 (November 7, 1969):727.

21. Karl Deutsch, *The Nerves of Government* (New York: Free Press, 1963), p. 236. © 1963 by The Free Press of Glencoe, a division of The Macmillan Company.

22. Stanley Milgram, "Some Conditions of Obedience and Disobedience to Authority," *International Journal of Psychiatry* (1960), pp. 259–76.

23. Perry London, *Behavioral Control* (New York: Harper & Row, 1969), p. 222.

24. Brad Darrach, "Meet Shaky, the First Electronic Person," *Life,* 69, no. 21(1970):68.

25. *Ibid.*

26. *Ibid.*

27. "Test Tube Baby Research Called Unethical," *Milwaukee Journal,* October 18, 1971.

28. *Science,* 168, no. 3935 (May 29, 1970):1076. Copyright © 1970 by the American Association for the Advancement of Science.

29. "Team Isolated Single Gene," *Milwaukee Journal,* Sunday, November 23, 1969, Part I.

30. E. Adamson Hoebel, *The Law of Primitive Man* (Cambridge, Mass.: Harvard University Press, 1954).

CHAPTER IV

1. José Ortega y Gasset, *The Dehumanization of Art* (New York: Doubleday & Co., 1956), p. 117.

2. Wilhelm Worringer, *Abstraction and Empathy* (New York: International Universities Press, 1953), p. 29.

3. Heinrich Wölfflin, *Principles of Art History* (New York: Dover Publications, 1932), pp. 14–16.

4. Daniel-Henry Kahnweiler, *The Rise of Cubism* (New York: Wittenborn, Schultz, 1949), p. 12.

5. Ortega y Gasset, *Dehumanization of Art,* p. 43.

6. Piet Mondrian, "The New Plastic Approach to Painting," in *Dictionary of Abstract Painting,* ed. Michel Seuphor (New York: Tudor Publishing Co., 1957), p. 103.

7. Arthur Drexler, *Ludwig Mies van der Rohe,* Masters of World Architecture Series (New York: Braziller, 1960), p. 24.

8. Walter Gropius, *The New Architecture and the Bauhaus* (Cambridge, Mass.: M.I.T. Press, 1965), p. 39.

9. Sigfried Giedion, *Space, Time and Architecture* (Cambridge, Mass.: Harvard University Press, 1967), p. 848.

10. Albert Einstein and Leopold Infeld, *The Evolution of Physics* (New York: Simon & Schuster, 1961), pp. 244–45, 297.

11. Jung, *Modern Man,* p. 179.

12. Amitai Etzioni, *Modern Organizations* (Englewood Cliffs, N.J.: Prentice-Hall, 1964), chaps. 3–5.

13. Paul Tillich, *The Courage to Be* (New Haven: Yale University Press, 1952), p. 61.

14. Jaspers, *Reason and Existenz,* p. 23.

15. Martin Buber, *Between Man and Man* (Boston: Beacon Press, 1955), p. 70.

16. Geoffrey Scott, *The Architecture of Humanism* (New York: Doubleday Anchor, 1956), p. 19.

17. Nan Fairbrother, *Men and Gardens* (New York: Alfred A. Knopf, 1956), chap. 8.

18. George R. Collins, *Antonio Gaudí,* Masters of World Architecture Series (New York: Braziller, 1960), p. 19.

19. Peter Blake, *Le Corbusier, Architecture and Form* (Baltimore, Penguin Books, 1964), p. 11.

20. Frank Lloyd Wright, "Education and Art in Behalf of Life," *Arts in Society* (University of Wisconsin, January, 1958), pp. 5–11.

21. Grady Clay, "Remembered Landscapes," in Paul Shepard and Daniel McKinley, eds., *The Subversive Science* (Boston: Houghton-Mifflin, 1968), p. 188.

22. Mondrian, "New Plastic Approach," p. 100.

23. William H. Masters and Virginia E. Johnson, *Human Sexual Response* (Boston: Little, Brown, 1966).

24. Theodore Roszak, *The Making of a Counter Culture* (New York: Doubleday & Co., 1969).

25. Charles A. Reich, *The Greening of America* (New York: Bantam Books, 1970), p. 285.

26. Michael Novak, *A Theology for Radical Politics* (New York: Herder & Herder, 1969).

27. "The Vietnam Vogue," *Newsweek,* July 12, 1971, p. 58.

28. Miguel de Unamuno, *The Tragic Sense of Life* (New York: Dover Publications, 1954), p. 115.

29. Louis A. Gottschalk and Mansell E. Pattison, "Psychiatric Perspectives on T-Groups and the Laboratory Movement: An Overview," *American Journal of Psychiatry,* 126, no. 6 (December, 1969):833–39.

30. Carl Rogers, "The T-Group Comes of Age," *Psychology Today,* 3, no. 7 (December, 1969):27.

31. *Ibid.,* p. 30.

32. *Ibid.,* p. 31.

33. Gottschalk and Pattison, "Psychiatric Perspectives."

34. Robert T. Golembiewski, "The Laboratory Approach to Organization Change: Schema of a Method," *Public Administration Review,* 27, no. 3 (September, 1967).

35. *Life,* "The Youth Communes," photographs by John Olson, 67, no. 3 (July 18, 1969):21. *Life* Magazine, © 1969 Time Inc.

36. William Hedgepeth and Dennis Stock, *The Alternative: Communal Life in New America* (New York: Macmillan, 1970), pp. 156, 163.

37. Rosabeth Moss Kanter, "Communes: Why and How They

Are Formed and Which Are Likely to Make It and Why," *Psychology Today,* 4, no. 2 (1970):56.

38. Bernhard-Karl, Duke of Saxe-Weimar-Eisenach, "Travels Through North America," 1825–26, in *Land of the Long Horizons,* ed. Walter Havighurst (New York: Coward-McCann, 1960), pp. 230–31.

39. Laurence Oliphant, "Minnesota and the Far West," 1855, in Havighurst, *Land of the Long Horizons,* pp. 296–97.

40. *Fortune,* February, 1970. See especially Sanford Rose, "The Economics of Environmental Quality," p. 120.

41. Sharp, "Technological Innovation."

42. Roszak, *Making of a Counter Culture,* p. 245.

43. "Reuss Sparks Call for Decade Dedicated to Cleanup" (Pledge of William Steiger), *Milwaukee Journal,* Sunday, December 21, 1969, Part I.

44. David Gumpert, "The New Pioneers," *Wall Street Journal,* 51, no. 189(1971).

45. Shepard and McKinley, *Subversive Science.*

CHAPTER V

1. Jaspers, *Reason and Existenz,* p. 62.

2. Alvin W. Gouldner, *The Coming Crisis of Western Sociology* (New York: Basic Books, 1970).

3. *Newsletter* of the American Anthropological Association, 12, no. 4(1971).

4. John W. Bennett, "Objectivity and Commitment," *Symposium MS, Anthropologists and Their Constituency,* American Ethnological Society (April, 1971), p. 6.

5. Ortega y Gasset, "The Self and the Other," *The Dehumanization of Art and Other Writings on Art and Culture.*

6. Søren Kierkegaard, *Fear and Trembling; and The Sickness Unto Death* (New York: Doubleday Anchor, 1955).

7. George Herbert Mead, *The Social Psychology of George Herbert Mead,* ed. Anselm Strauss (Chicago: University of Chicago Press, Phoenix Books, 1934).

8. Charles H. Cooley, *Human Nature and the Social Order* (New York: Scribner, 1902), p. 218.

9. Mead, *Social Psychology,* p. 218.

10. George H. Bishop, "Feedback Through the Environment as an Analog of Brain Functioning," *Self-Organizing Systems,* Yovits and Cameron, eds. (New York: Macmillan, 1960). See also Karl U. Smith, "Environmental Research and Sensory Feedback Analysis of Behavior," *Proceedings of the Institute of Environmental Scientists* (Chicago, 1962), pp. 353–68.

11. Edward A. Feigenbaum, "An Experimental Course in Simulation of Cognitive Processes," *Behavioral Science,* 7, no. 2 (1962).
See also Wayne A. Wickelgren, "A Simulation Program for Concept Attainment by Conservative Focusing," *Behavioral Science,* 7, no. 2(1962).

12. Tillich, *Courage to Be,* pp. 86–103, 113–51.

13. Kierkegaard, *Fear and Trembling,* p. 162.

14. Alan Chester Kerckhoff and Thomas C. McCormick, "Marginal Status and Marginal Personality," *Social Forces,* 37(1959):196–202.

15. Jean Paul Sartre, *Existential Psychoanalysis* (New York: Philosophical Library, 1953), pp. 203–60.
Søren Kierkegaard, "Shadowgraphs," in *Either/Or* (New York: Doubleday Anchor, 1959), 1:161–213.

16. Ortega y Gasset, "In Search of Goethe from Within," *Dehumanization of Art,* pp. 121–60.

17. Harry F. Harlow, Robert O. Dodsworth and Margaret K. Harlow, "Total Social Isolation in Monkeys," *Proceedings of the National Academy of Sciences,* 54, no. 1 (July, 1965): 90–97. See also Harry F. Harlow, Guy L. Rowland and Gary A. Griffin, "The Effect of Total Social Deprivation on the Development of Monkey Behavior," *Psychiatric Research Report 19,* American Psychiatric Association (December, 1964), pp. 116–35.

18. David A. Hamburg and Donald T. Lunde, "Sex Hormones in the Development of Sex Differences in Human Behavior," in *The Development of Sex Differences,* ed. Eleanor E. Maccoby (Stanford U. Press, 1966), pp. 1–24.

19. T. Ayllon, E. Haughton and H. O. Osmond, "Chronic Anorexia: A Behavior Problem," *Canadian Psychiatric Association Journal,* 9, no. 2 (April, 1964): 147–54.

20. D. O. Hebb, *Organization of Behavior* (New York: Wiley, Science Editions, 1961), pp. 144, 146.

21. B. F. Skinner, *Beyond Freedom and Dignity* (New York: Alfred A. Knopf, 1971), p. 167.

22. Donald W. MacKinnon, "What Makes a Person Creative?" in *Psychology in Administration,* Timothy W. Costello and Sheldon S. Zalkind, eds. (Englewood Cliffs, N.J.: Prentice-Hall, 1963), pp. 416–21.
    See also Morris I. Stein and Shirley Heinze, *Creativity and the Individual* (Chicago: University of Chicago Graduate School of Business, 1960).
    See also J. W. Getzels and P. W. Jackson, *Creativity and Intelligence* (New York: Wiley, 1961).

23. Allan Nevins, "Henry Ford: A Complex Man," in *World War I and the Twenties,* Robert G. Athearn (New York: Dell, 1963), 13:1165–66.

24. Kamla Chowdhry and Theodore M. Newcomb, "The Relative Abilities of Leaders and Non-Leaders to Estimate Opinions

of Their Own Groups," in *Small Groups,* A. Paul Hare, Edgar F. Borgatta and Robert F. Bales, eds. (New York: Alfred A. Knopf, 1965).

25. K. E. Read, "Leadership and Consensus in a New Guinea Society," *American Anthropologist,* 61, no. 3(June, 1959): 433–34. Reproduced by permission of the American Anthropological Society.

26. Richard Hofstadter, *The American Political Tradition* (New York: Vintage, 1958), p. 336.

27. Anthony Storr, "The Man," in *Churchill Revised: A Critical Assessment,* A. J. P. Taylor, Robert Rhodes James, J. H. Plumb, Basil Liddell Hart and Anthony Storr (New York: Dial, 1969), pp. 230–69.

28. Arnold Toynbee, *A Study of History,* abr. D. C. Somervell (New York: Oxford University Press, 1947), pp. 217–30.

29. Hofstadter, *American Political Tradition,* p. 351.

30. T. E. Hulme, *Speculations* (New York: Harcourt, Brace & Co., Harvest, 1924), p. 117.

31. Herbert Read, *Education Through Art* (New York: Pantheon, 1945), pp. 89–90.

32. Michael Balint, *Thrills and Regressions* (New York: International Universities Press, 1959), pp. 26–31.

33. Henry Miller, *Tropic of Cancer* (New York: Grove, 1961), p. 253.

34. Ortega y Gasset, *Revolt of the Masses,* p. 63.

35. Peirce, *Chance, Love and Logic,* pp. 72–73.

CHAPTER VI

1. Karl von Frisch, *The Dance Language and Orientation of*

Bees (Cambridge, Mass.: Harvard University Press, 1969), chap. 4.

2. Hebb, *Organization of Behavior,* pp. 232–33.

3. Ernest T. Gilliard, *Birds of Paradise and Bowerbirds* (Garden City, N.Y.: Natural History Press, 1969), pp. 49–60.

4. D'Arcy Thompson, *Growth and Form* (Cambridge, 1968).

5. John Dewey, *How We Think* (New York: D. C. Heath & Co., 1939), p. 12.

6. *Ibid.,* p. 107.

7. Costello and Zalkind, *Psychology in Administration* (Prentice-Hall), pp. 340–42.

8. *Ibid.,* pp. 343–50.

9. Simon, *New Science of Management Decision,* p. 3.

10. Hans Selye, *The Stress of Life* (New York: McGraw-Hill Paperbacks, 1956), p. 297.

11. Jerome S. Bruner, "On Perceptual Readiness," *Psychological Review,* 64, no. 2 (1957):123–52.

12. J. P. Guilford, *The Nature of Human Intelligence* (New York: McGraw-Hill, 1967), chaps. 6–8.

13. Anthony F. Wallace, "Revitalization Movements," *American Anthropologist,* 53(1956):264–81.

14. Hebb, *Organization of Behavior,* pp. 6, 144.

15. Frank Lloyd Wright, "The Concept and the Plan," 1928, *Architectural Record,* in *F. L. Wright, Writings and Buildings,* Edgar Kaufmann and Ben Raeburn, eds. (New York: Meridian Books, 1960), p. 221. By permission of The Frank Lloyd Wright Foundation. Copyright © 1960 by The Frank Lloyd Wright Foundation.

16. Harold E. Johnson, *Jean Sibelius* (New York: Alfred A. Knopf, 1959), p. 188.

17. M. Sherif, *The Psychology of Social Norms* (New York: Harper & Co., 1936).

18. Victor A. Thompson, *Modern Organization* (New York: Alfred A. Knopf, 1965), chap. 8.

19. Edward Gibbon, *The Decline and Fall of the Roman Empire* (New York: Peter Fenelon Collier, 1776–88).
    Oswald Spengler, *The Decline of the West* (New York: Alfred A. Knopf, 1917).
    Brooks Adams, *The Law of Civilization and Decay* (New York: Alfred A. Knopf, 1943).

20. Wallace, "Revitalization Movements."

21. Charles S. Peirce, "The Essentials of Pragmatism," 1905, in *Philosophical Writings of Peirce,* ed. Justus Buchler (New York: Dover Publications, 1955), p. 251.

22. Jean Paul Sartre, *Saint Genêt* (New York: Mentor Press, 1963), p. 628.

23. Toynbee, *Study of History,* p. 332.

24. George C. Vaillant, *Aztecs of Mexico* (New York: Doubleday & Co., 1947), chap. 14.

25. Michael Lewis, *The Navy of Britain* (Great Britain: Unwin Bros., 1948), pp. 479–82, 491–95.

26. *Ibid.,* p. 481.

27. Robert V. Bruce, *Lincoln and the Tools of War* (New York: Bobbs-Merrill, 1956), pp. 69–71.

28. Barbara W. Tuchman, *The Guns of August* (New York: Dell, 1962), pp. 55, 216.

29. Corelli Barnett, *The Desert Generals* (London: William Kimber & Co., 1960), pp. 100–105.

30. James Leasor, *Singapore: The Battle That Changed the World* (New York: Doubleday & Co., 1968), p. 11.

31. "Winston Leonard Spencer Churchill," *Biographical Memoirs of Fellows of the Royal Society,* 12 (London: Royal Society, Burlington House, 1966), p. 63.

32. William Schofield, *Psychotherapy: The Purchase of Friendship* (Englewood Cliffs, N.J.: Prentice-Hall, 1964), p. 2.

33. Leo Srole *et al., Mental Health in the Metropolis* (New York: McGraw-Hill, 1962), chap. 8.

34. H. J. Eysenck, "The Effect of Psychotherapy," *Handbook of Abnormal Psychology* (New York: Basic Books, 1961), chap. 18.
See also Teodoro Ayllon and Jack Michael, "The Psychiatric Nurse as a Behavioral Engineer," *Journal of Experimental Analysis of Behavior,* 2(1959):323–34.

35. Jeanne Miller and Bernard J. James, "Social Work Practice and Community Mental Health," *Community Mental Health Journal,* 8, no. 3 (1972), 178–88.

36. Hebb, *Organization of Behavior,* p. 263.
See also Linus Pauling, "Orthomolecular Psychiatry," *Science,* 160, no. 3825(April 19, 1968):265–71.
See also David Rosenthal, "A Program of Research on Heredity in Schizophrenia," *Behavioral Science,* 16, no. 3(May, 1971):191–201.

37. Aldo Leopold, in Frank Fraser Darling, "A Wider Environment of Ecology and Conservation," *Daedalus,* 96, no. 4 (Fall, 1967):1004.

38. Stephen B. Shepard, "What Technology Has Wrought, It Can Undo," *Newsweek,* October 23, 1971, p. 13.

39. "Delaware: Nature Over Industry," *Newsweek,* July 5, 1971, pp. 55–56.

40. Barry Commoner, *The Closing Circle* (New York: Alfred A. Knopf, 1971), chap. 9.

41. Samuel H. Ordway, Jr., "Possible Limits of Raw Material Consumption," in *Man's Role in Changing the Face of the Earth,* ed. William L. Thomas, Jr. (Chicago: University of Chicago Press, 1970) 2: 993.
See also Commoner, *Closing Circle,* pp. 161–66.

42. R. H. Whittaker, "A Consideration of Climax Theory: The Climax as a Population and Pattern," *Ecological Monographs,* 23, no. 1(1953):41–78.

43. Jay Forrester, *World Dynamics* (Wright-Allen Press, 1971).
See also E. O. Attinger, ed., *Global Systems Dynamics* (New York: Wiley-Interscience, 1971).
See also Ordway, "Possible Limits," p. 994.

44. George Peter Murdock, *Ethnographic Atlas* (Pittsburgh: University of Pittsburgh Press, 1967).
See also Robert B. Textor, *A Cross-Cultural Summary* (New Haven: Human Relations Area File Press, 1967).

45. Commoner, *Closing Circle,* p. 175.
See also Lynton Keith Caldwell, *Environment,* section 1 (Garden City, N.Y.: Natural History Press, 1970).

46. Robert McC. Netting, "The Ecological Approach in Cultural Study," *An Addison-Wesley Module* (Reading, Mass.: Addison-Wesley, 1971).

47. Sir George Stapledon, *Human Ecology,* ed. Robert Waller, published posthumously (London: Charles Knight & Co., 1971), p. 109.

48. Miller, *Assault on Privacy.*

A NOTE ABOUT THE AUTHOR

Bernard James received his Ph.D. in cultural anthropology from the University of Wisconsin in 1954. He is now Professor of Anthropology and Director of The Center for Advanced Study in Organization Science at the University of Wisconsin–Milwaukee. He is also Consulting Editor of the journal *Arts in Society*.

A NOTE ON THE TYPE

The text of this book was set in a face called Times Roman, designed by Stanley Morison for *The Times* (London) and first introduced by that newspaper in 1932.

Among typographers and designers of the twentieth century, Stanley Morison has been a strong forming influence, as typographical advisor to the English Monotype Corporation, as a director of two distinguished English publishing houses, and as a writer of sensibility, erudition, and keen practical sense.

Composed, printed and bound by
The Colonial Press Inc., Clinton, Mass.

Typography and binding design by Virginia Tan

DATE DUE